This is a beautiful portrayal of the special role ... person's life. It is deeply honest and courageous ... only to those who are seeking to find such a soul ... feel the calling to guide and encourage another . ...ey. I found it a great privilege to be invited into this journey, from its touching and tentative beginnings, to the profound depth of Godly influence which is shared so sensitively.

Dr Carol Preston, counsellor and author of seven historical fiction works, including *Mary's Guardian, Charlotte's Angel* and *Tangled Secrets.*

Soul friendship is a very under-emphasised resource of Christian discipleship, particularly for Christian leaders. Jo-Anne has written honestly, beautifully, sensitively and powerfully. I trust this will be an encouragement to many of us to further seek similar enriching, God-blessed relationships.

Dr Keith Farmer, mentor and past Principal, Australian College of Ministries

Soul Friend is a celebration of a spiritual friendship which began in the context of fulfilling the requirements of a program of formation for ministry but unfolded in a wonderful way to go far beyond that, showing how, under God, such a relationship can become mutual and enduring.

Bishop John Noble

Beautifully written, this honest and insightful memoir is an inspiring celebration of the ancient art of spiritual companionship. If you don't have a mentor, this book will make you want one; if you do, it opens up new possibilities for going deeper and further.

Dr Rick Lewis, author of *Mentoring Matters*

This book embraces the outworking of a God-given dream for Jo-Anne. A story of transparency, honesty and vulnerability as Jo-Anne weaves her journey with that of her soul friend. In my twenty years relationship, Jo-Anne has always passionately communicated her desire to search for a deeper and more intimate spiritual life. This book *Soul Friend* is another phase in this journey. It will cause you as the reader to reflect on your own faith journey.

Les Scarborough, John Mark Ministries, mentor, trainer, consultant and spiritual retreat facilitator

Soul Friend
Published by Even Before Publishing, a division of Wombat Books.
P. O. Box 1519, Capalaba Qld 4157
www.evenbeforepublishing.com
www.wombatbooks.com.au

© Jo-Anne Berthelsen 2012
Cover by Even Before Publishing
Layout by Even Before Publishing

National Library of Australia Cataloguing-in-Publication entry
Author: Berthelsen, Jo-Anne.
Title: Soul friend : the story of a shared spiritual journey /
               Jo-Anne Berthelsen.
ISBN: 9781922074492 (pbk.)
Notes: Includes bibliographical references.
Subjects: Berthelsen, Jo-Anne.
               Spiritual life.
               Friendship.
Dewey Number: 248.4

All Scripture quotations are taken from the HOLY BIBLE, NEW
INTERNATIONAL VERSION. Copyright © 1973, 1978, 1984 International
Bible Society. Used by permission of Zondervan Bible Publishers.

Soul Friend
The story of a
shared spiritual
journey

Jo-Anne Berthelsen

Even Before Publishing

Australia

CONTENTS

FOR JOY, WITH LOVE

Introduction

My journey in writing *Soul Friend* has been an interesting and challenging one. It was begun after much thought and prayer, as well as consultation with my spiritual friend Joy. While the idea for this book came to me very clearly around two years ago, I was hesitant to embark on it for two reasons. Firstly, I knew I would have to expose many of my innermost thoughts and struggles over the past fifteen years, since beginning to meet with Joy. Unlike novels, there is nowhere to hide in a work of non-fiction such as this! But secondly, I knew I would have to deal honestly with some parts of my journey that involved others – and I did not want to offend or misrepresent these men or women in any way. My aim in my writing and speaking has always been to build others up and not tear down, but if I have hurt anyone by what I have written here or what I have omitted, I apologise. This is my story from my perspective of the last fifteen years of my journey and Joy's loving ministry to me in that time. Others may see things differently, but I have tried my best to write with honesty, sensitivity and grace.

Yet I also approached the writing of this book with great joy for three reasons. Firstly, I wanted to honour Joy for the many hours spent talking with and praying for me over the years, for her continued belief in me and her ongoing support in the different forms of ministry I have undertaken in this time. Secondly, I hoped through this book to encourage others to engage in similar supportive relationships, either as the one offering the spiritual friendship and support or as the one seeking such a friendship. And thirdly, by being as honest and transparent as I could, I hoped God would use my words to minister to any readers going through similar life experiences.

I hope I have succeeded in writing the book I believe God wanted written. I thank my dear friend Joy Crawford for her support throughout and her preparedness to have our private conversations and something of her own journey exposed for all to see in this way. I thank my two faithful manuscript readers and editors, Jane Louise and Lorene Noble for their time and effort on my behalf yet again, and also Joy Crawford herself, as well as my friend Ruth Allan, for their valuable comments. And lastly, thank you to Rochelle Manners from Even Before Publishing and editorial assistant Lynne Stringer for their efforts in bringing this book to fruition.

God bless you as you read. May you be drawn closer to the Lord, the perfect Soul Friend, and find strength and encouragement for your own spiritual journey.

Jo-Anne Berthelsen

SOUL FRIEND

Chapter One

Making the Connection

I sat with the phone cradled in my hand, repeating over and over in my mind the words I planned to say. I hated making phone calls at the best of times and this one was proving particularly difficult. It seemed so impertinent and self-centred to ask someone to invest time and energy into meeting with me on a regular basis. Should I perhaps not phone after all? Should I leave it and ask someone else I knew better?

I looked at the number I had scribbled down yet again, trying to bring to mind the face of my friend I had not seen for almost two years. We were part way between friend and acquaintance really— two people who had been thrown together in an unusual context for a brief period only. Would she even remember me? I knew her life was full and her skills much in demand. Surely she would feel I was being presumptuous expecting her to invest herself in me to such an extent?

Yet she was the best possible person I could think of to be my spiritual mentor. I had loved how she had led our small group with such sensitivity at the prayer training school we had both attended. I had admired her gentle manner and the warmth and love that exuded from her to each member of our group. We were different ages, with different experiences of life and church. Two were single and two married—and on top of that, one was blind. But Joy welcomed us all, accepting us where and how we were.

Joy lived up to her name. She loved to sing and worship God with all her heart and soul and her joy was infectious. But she knew how to weep with us too, as we shared our broken souls during those three weeks together. She listened to God's Spirit and reached out with healing love in ways I would never have dreamt of. We were on sacred ground—and I treasured each moment.

I left that training school determined to learn how to lead groups in that same warm, sensitive way. I knew I did not have Joy's experience and depth of knowledge of the things of God, but one day I hoped with all my heart I would.

Now here was my opportunity to take a step towards doing just that. It was February 1996, and I was about to begin my second year at theological college, fulfilling a long-held dream to train fulltime for some form of ministry. Our college course required every student to meet with a mentor on a weekly basis for one hour in order to monitor our spiritual development and to ensure we progressed both academically and spiritually. I had enjoyed a good mentoring relationship with someone from our own church the previous year, but, by mutual agreement, we had decided I needed to find someone right outside our own church community with different insights and experiences.

Taking my courage in both hands, at last I dialled the number.

'H-h-hello, Joy,' I stuttered when I heard her friendly voice on the other end of the line. 'I'm not sure if you remember me, but my name's Jo-Anne Berthelsen. We met almost two years ago at the prayer training school in Wahroonga.'

'Of *course* I remember you, Jo-Anne! How lovely to hear your voice again. Oh, how *are* you? It's been such a long time!'

I breathed a sigh of relief. Joy was so warm and approachable, just as I had remembered her to be. We chatted on for a while and then I knew it was time to put my request to her.

'Joy, I need to have a spiritual mentor who is happy to meet with me on a regular basis—it's part of the requirements of my college course. I'm supposed to meet with this person one hour a week, but it can be two hours a fortnight, if that's more convenient. It's no problem if you don't want to or don't have time to, but I was wondering if you might consider being that person for me.'

It was out there now—the words could not be taken back. I braced myself for the pregnant pause I was sure would come. I knew Joy well enough to sense she would want to think about how to let me down as gently as possible.

I was not at all prepared for what I heard next.

'Oh, I'd love to do that—how wonderful! Thank you for asking me.'

Now there was indeed a very long a pause as I tried to gather my scattered wits. My hand went limp and I almost dropped the phone. Had Joy *really* said yes? Surely it couldn't be so easy?

'Would you ... would you really, Joy?' I managed to gasp out at last. 'I mean ... you don't *have* to.'

'Yes, I know, but I'd feel very privileged to be able to do that for you, Jo-Anne,' I heard her respond. 'Of course, I don't know all that's required, but perhaps you can explain that to me when we meet. To be honest, I'm not sure I'm very comfortable with the word "mentor" at all, but anyway, we can talk about that too. So ... when would you like to catch up?'

Soon it was all arranged. I was to drive up to her home in the Blue Mountains west of Sydney the following Monday morning. And after stuttering out my thanks, I put the phone down and stayed where I was for some time, still too shocked to move.

'She said yes! She said yes!' my spirit sang. And even then, I knew Joy was the person God had chosen to speak into my life during the next few challenging years as I completed college and headed into pastoral ministry. At that point, I could not see beyond that. Yet our journey together was to last much longer and bear more fruit than I would ever have envisaged in my wildest imaginings.

Chapter Two

The Journey Begins

Early that next Monday morning, as arranged, I found myself heading west along the M4 up into the Blue Mountains. I was about to visit Joy's home for the first time and I was looking forward to the experience so much.

On that day—and many others over the following years—this drive away from the city became a wonderful provision for me in itself and part of the healing impact of my visits to Joy. It gave me space to process the events of the previous day at church and the week leading up to it and begin to gain a better perspective on things. I would think too about what I needed to discuss with Joy in our time together. And, except for rainy days when the mists enveloped all but the houses and vegetation closest to the road, the amazing glimpses of seemingly endless, tree-covered ranges and valleys soothed my spirit and enlarged my vision. Compared with the splendour of God's creation, what were my little fears and concerns? Nothing was impossible for my great God.

As instructed, I turned right at a service station and headed downhill until I reached a left hand turn on the edge of bushland. I drove slowly—I knew I must be close now. But when I approached Joy's street and searched for the right house, shyness began to overtake me. What if our time together did not go as well as I hoped? What if Joy regretted she had agreed to meet with me? Well, there was nothing for it. I had to go through with this first meeting at least.

I parked the car and took my time walking up the driveway. Joy's house was painted a smoky green and blended in beautifully with the surrounding trees and shrubs. It was not new by any means but gave out a sense of comfort and unpretentiousness that appealed to me. As I climbed the front steps, I noticed how extensive her garden was and discovered later that the property covered two housing allotments. It had been purchased many years before with an inheritance Joy's husband, David, had received and from the outset was intended not only for personal use but also for church camps and retreats. Later, when David retired from ministry, it had become the family home.

I reached the front door and rang the bell. And as I waited, I feasted my eyes on the beautiful, purple flowering creeper that wound itself around the railings of the wooden deck and the colourful blossoms on the nearby shrubs. Already, God seemed to be reaching out to me through the beauty of creation. Then the door opened and there was Joy, just as I remembered her.

'Oh, it's so good to see you again, Jo-Anne!' she greeted me in her gentle, musical voice. 'Welcome to our place—do come in!'

She reached up and gave me a warm hug, then stepped back and looked at me.

'How *are* you? Are you a little tired after your trip? Let me get you a cup of tea—or perhaps you'd like to freshen up first?'

I looked down at Joy's diminutive figure, her short, grey hair framing a face alight with warmth and love. And I knew again I could trust her with all the turmoil and ups and downs of my life.

She directed me to the bathroom and headed to the kitchen to make our tea. I soon followed her and found her husband there, hovering in the background and listening to ABC radio. David greeted me in his beautiful, gentlemanly manner, remembering me from our first prayer training school. He was tall, slim and upright, and reminded me of my grandfather in earlier years. Yet his eyes twinkled and the witty, insightful comments he made about what he had heard on the radio showed an intelligence and sense of humour that must have served him well during his years in ministry. David graciously slipped away elsewhere then, as he did most days I visited, in order for Joy to focus her attention on me.

'What would you like, Jo-Anne? I have some Earl Grey tea or ordinary tea, if you'd prefer. And I have some Lady Grey as well that a friend gave me. Would you like to try it?'

From that day on, it became a tradition for Joy to serve me either Earl Grey or Lady Grey tea, which we would carry into her small study. But on this first day, Joy conducted me first of all on a brief tour of the property. On the back porch, I saw numerous seedlings waiting to be planted out in the already overflowing garden. I could tell even then how much Joy loved her garden and how vital it was as a source of refreshment and peace for her. I wandered along the small pathways, admiring the beauty of the eclectic mix of old-fashioned English cottage garden plants and Australian natives, many whose names I did not know. Joy seemed to be an expert on such things, however, identifying various plants for me and often commenting on who had given them to her. And when I admired one particular plant with large, dark leaves and purple flowers that seemed to have popped up willy-nilly in different spots, she offered to grow some from cuttings for me.

'It's a very old-fashioned plant,' she explained. 'I don't know its botanical name, but it's called "honesty"! When the flower dies off, these beautiful, opaque seed pods form on the long stems. Then you rub the sides of the pods and remove the seeds to keep for another time, but the rest makes a lovely dried arrangement.'

Then and there, I wanted some for my garden. This plant seemed a fitting image for the honesty I sensed in Joy and wanted in every facet of my life as well, including my faith. And it did not take many meetings to discover that integrity and authenticity were indeed traits she prized.

We walked on past the small fishpond to the self-contained flat known as *The Quiet House*. Joy told me this was available for day-long group retreats or for those wishing to make a personal retreat of their own for a period of time. And, at the rear of the property, I was shown a tiny, brown, rustic chapel built by David, with room for about half a dozen people, and was told how Christian friends from different traditions came together there one morning a week to share in a largely silent time of prayer. I drank in the peace and holiness of that sacred space, as my mind pictured the Catholic priest, the Baptist minister and the hermit seated alongside Joy and David in unity of spirit.

We returned to the kitchen by way of Joy's large vegetable garden, where care had been taken to use organic methods of cultivation and where pumpkin vines wandered wherever they wished in a way that seemed so right. As with many other residents of the Blue Mountains, Joy and David were keen to work with nature and not against it, helping to conserve our precious resources. Joy loved every corner of her garden, it was easy to see.

In the kitchen, she arranged our tea on a pretty tray, along with a small plate of biscuits, and carried it to the study. Then she closed the door to ensure my complete privacy.

In some strange way, I felt I had come home.

I curled up in the comfortable lounge opposite Joy and leant back against the cushions, sipping my tea. Through the nearby windows, I could see the flowering shrubs I had noticed on my arrival and the taller trees beyond. Beneath the windows and within my reach was a small, rosewood table with a candle on it and a vase of freshly picked flowers. A bookshelf filled a large part of the wall opposite, containing a fascinating mixture of books on prayer, the spiritual life, counselling and worship, several biographies, the writings of some of the great

8

mystics, various volumes of poetry, and a few novels by Christian authors such as Elizabeth Goudge and Madeleine L'Engle. Straight away, I felt I wanted to delve into them all and explore their wonderful richness and variety.

I finished my tea and Joy lit the candle as a sign of God's presence with us. Then silence fell. This silence was in itself a precious gift and became something I treasured so much during many future visits. I heard later how Joy had first learnt the value of silence with God and of listening for God's voice when she and David were introduced to the ministry of Camp Farthest Out, a movement founded by Glenn Clark and brought to Australia in 1959.[1] Such experiences had brought a depth and richness to Joy's spirituality that I admired and wanted to explore for myself. I sensed there were many new understandings waiting for me to discover with Joy—including things about myself and my responses to situations inside and outside of ministry.

Joy had been born and raised in church circles and had met David at their church's large and vibrant youth group. They were married in David's final year at theological college, after which they accepted a call to minister at Manly and then Miranda in Sydney's south, followed by Bondi and then Malabar, where they stayed for twenty-one years. During these years at Malabar, they had been part of establishing a 'common purse' community within the wider body of the church, living and sharing all things together. Later still, they were called to an inner city church at Surry Hills, a ministry that required them to develop new ways of caring for the many marginalised people around them. Together, they had been unafraid to push boundaries in all the churches where they had served and to establish creative, grassroots ministries that seemed almost ahead of their time. I had seen glimpses in our small group of some of the things Joy had gleaned from her vast ministry experience—and I wanted to find out much more.

On that first morning, however, before our journey together could begin, I needed to explain the expectations of our college to her. We had agreed to meet for two hours every second Monday morning for the rest of the college year, but I was also required to formulate some personal goals to work towards during our times together. Also, each semester Joy was required to sign a form, declaring we had met as stated, and comment on my progress towards achieving my goals. Yet I soon discovered some compromise would be needed in this area. Helping me work out personal goals and strategies was not how Joy operated.

'I'm not even sure I'm comfortable with the term "mentor",' she confessed. 'I much prefer the term "spiritual friend" or "spiritual companion". To me, a mentor indicates someone more highly qualified or superior—and that's not how I regard our relationship. Yes, I've been involved in quite a few different ministries over the years and I'm happy to share what I can with you, but I'm sure you have things to teach me as well. I feel too that mentoring is a more prescribed process, whereas being a spiritual friend or companion is more organic and "whole of life". I see it as a relationship between two living, growing human beings in which one helps the other discern God's movement in his or her life.'

I understood her reservations and did not feel they would cause any difficulty either for college or for me. Besides, as far as I was concerned, the college requirements were of secondary importance. We would meet as required and I would devise my own goals, as well as the strategies for reaching these. And yes, we would talk about matters to do with these goals, but we would not be slavish about it. Of primary consideration for me was that we follow God's agenda. And, in the process, I hoped to learn all I could from Joy and imbibe more and more of the godly wisdom and beautiful, warm spirituality I saw in her. God had brought us together, I believed, and my task was to have eyes to see and ears to hear what I needed to learn in this relationship.

I suspect Joy may have felt bewildered at times with the torrent of information I dumped on her that first morning. In my busyness and my self-focused mindset, I had not considered the fact that she might be unfamiliar with the way our theological college functioned. On top of that, I belonged to a different denomination from her, one much less structured in many ways, with a strong emphasis on the 'priesthood of all believers'. Our members were encouraged to become involved in all aspects of ministry, including leadership as church elders or deacons or ministry coordinators. After all, we could trace our roots back to American Frontier days when the founders of our movement had wanted to throw off what they saw to be the shackles of the 'Old World' and the traditional ways of 'doing' church, in order to return to the simple faith and practices of the New Testament.

But, beyond that, our own local church was unique in many ways. An interesting mixture of people attended our services—from the well-educated and highly paid, to those at the opposite end of the socio-economic scale. We numbered close to four hundred members and regular attendees at that point, with a large percentage coming from outside the immediate vicinity of the church. Many young people were drawn by the excellent music in our services and the quality of our pastoral team, while others loved the relevant, biblical preaching. But, as a church, we also tried to reach out to the needy in the Department of Housing accommodation in our local area—and that brought a different dimension again to our church's culture. Joy was warmed to hear about our ministries to these marginalised people, since this was familiar territory from her own days in Surry Hills. Yet much of what I told her with such enthusiasm about our church that morning was new and left her shaking her head in amazement.

Another factor I shared with her was that, in recent years in particular, our church had experienced the wave of renewal that was flowing through many churches at the time, bringing the more tangible presence and power of the Holy Spirit among us. We were on a journey together of trying to exercise the gifts of the Spirit with freedom, but also in a wise way that would bless and build up the body. It was an exciting time to be part of our church, although these things brought challenges as well, particularly for our leaders.

Joy was interested in everything I tried to explain to her. She marvelled at what God was doing amongst us and was delighted to find I was part of such a vibrant faith community.

'That's wonderful!' she would exclaim often. 'Thank you, Lord!'

As I noted her response and glimpsed from her perspective the richness of my experiences both at college and church, I realised afresh how blessed I was to be part of it all. But, on that first morning early in 1996, I also came to Joy with some pressing needs.

My first year at theological college had been exhilarating, but also exhausting. On first hearing I was heading for college, a wise friend had encouraged me merely to 'aim to pass'. He knew I was a perfectionist and would want to achieve constant high grades—and he was right. I could not seem to resign myself to putting half an effort into any assignment or task—and once I began to receive Distinctions and High Distinctions, I became reluctant to accept anything less. True, as a mature age student who had always liked studying, I enjoyed researching each subject and gaining more understanding, but pride and self-justification drove me too.

Along with that had come a demanding program of practical ministry in our church. Despite the many encouraging things happening amongst us, it had not been an easy year, especially for those of us involved in the area of prayer. On the whole, our leaders had dealt well with various aspects of renewal the Holy Spirit had brought into our midst—how to give and receive prophetic words in a way that built up the body, for example, and how to handle other manifestations of the Spirit. But there had been frustrations too for some members, several of whom had decided to leave because our church, in their opinion, was not embracing enough of the new things God was doing. At the same time, others were leaving because they felt we were embracing *too much* that was not godly at all. And since part of my ministry involved pastoral care, I felt caught up in this situation.

As well, our church had been working through the issue of women in leadership. The previous year, I had written to our ministers and elders, asking them whether we might be able to have a woman elder. This request was handled with sensitivity and a process had taken place in which I was involved to gauge members' opinions. This went well and in the end, the church elected its first female elder. But I had weathered some unexpected negativity from others in the process, which I found personally draining. As a result, I was feeling somewhat angry and depressed—even a little cynical—and also questioning whether there would ever be a place for me in any paid ministry role.

So I came to my first meeting with Joy a bundle of confusion, frustration, self-doubt and emotional exhaustion. I was wholeheartedly committed to God and to my college studies, yet ambivalent towards whether I should stay at our church or undertake my practical ministry elsewhere. I loved our church with a passion—perhaps too much so. But could God be showing me it was time to explore new territory where there might perhaps be fewer complex issues?

I needed someone to show me the way back to a place of rest with God—a place of joy and peace and hope for the future.

On that first day, I felt so relieved to be able to speak freely about these issues. With Joy, I sensed I could say whatever I liked and know I would still be loved and accepted. At times, I needed to explain some things about our church to her, since we came from different parts of the body of Christ, but she was not enmeshed with the people and issues there, nor did she have any agenda as far as either our church or college was concerned. Joy was there for me—and me alone. And that was a gift from God not to be taken lightly.

Joy saw the two main tasks of being a spiritual companion as creating a safe place for those who came and enabling them to feel heard. And on that first day, that was exactly what she did for me. For so long I had felt like a coiled spring, primed and ready for action at all times. But on that morning, something began to relax inside me. I, of course, did most of the talking, while Joy listened. Yet she did manage to make some gentle comments from time to time. And, much to her surprise and perhaps even embarrassment, I decided to record these in a journal I had brought with me.

'I don't want to forget anything you've said,' I told her. 'This way, I can think and pray about it again later.'

Joy seemed to feel she had said nothing profound or noteworthy, yet to me, many of the things I jotted down were precious pearls of wisdom I wanted to treasure. I was to write down many more in the months ahead—and also to hear some of them repeated, just when I needed to be reminded of them.

When we finished talking, our candle was still burning. As I sat staring into its flame, quietening my spirit and sensing the presence of God, Joy did the same. We sat in silence for several minutes, lost in that loving Presence. Neither of us felt forced to say anything. But eventually, Joy leant back with a sigh.

'Thank you, Lord,' she said.

It was all that was needed.

We checked the date for our next meeting before saying goodbye. Joy walked with me as far as her letterbox and held me close in a warm hug.

'Drive safely, dear friend,' she told me. 'Take care of yourself!'

Then she added some words I was to hear quite often—words written in the fourteenth century by Julian of Norwich but which now touched me profoundly:

'Remember, "*All shall be well, and all shall be well, and all manner of thing shall be well.*"²

CHAPTER THREE

EARLY STRUGGLES

I was to arrive at Joy's home as soon after nine as possible on each of the Monday mornings we were due to meet. That way, I could spend the rest of the day on college assignments or practical ministry. At times I felt weary as I prepared to leave for the trip up the mountains. Often I would have arrived home late from church the previous night, after talking and praying with people. Then it was often hard to unwind. Nevertheless, however tired I felt, I always set out with a sense of relief. Waiting for me in the mountains was a place where I could share from my heart and know I would be listened to. And, whether what I shared made sense or not, I knew Joy would accept me and pray for me in whatever way God led.

During the first few months we met together, it was often a rather doleful person who arrived on Joy's doorstep. In many ways, great things were still happening at our church. Also, I continued to do well at college. But the deep joy and peace I had had with God was taking a battering under the weight of my practical ministry responsibilities and the expectations I had of myself to do well in everything. Also, my frustration over some church issues continued to take their toll. Early that year, some words from Galatians 4 had greatly challenged me. There, Paul pleads with believers not to lose the freedom they have in Christ and to resist taking on the burden of obeying the law again. In verse 15, he asks them a simple question: *What has happened to all your joy?* That was a question I longed to answer for myself—and it seemed ironic that the very person God had provided to help me in this had been given that name.

Later I was to discover Joy's first name was in fact Winifred, in honour of her mother, but that she had always been called by her second name. Yet she had not always liked the name Joy and at one stage had wanted to change it. She had grown tired of people quoting the phrase 'Joy by name and Joy by nature' to her and felt it put too much pressure on her to be bright and joyful. But, long before we met, Joy had grown to appreciate it and would always welcome me with a warm smile, whatever else was happening in her life. Sometimes my visits would fall on the same day she and David held their early morning time of meditation in their small chapel.

'It's wonderful,' she would often tell me. 'One of us will read a passage of Scripture or some other text and then we simply sit together in God's presence. It's a very sweet time when our souls meet with God and one another.'

On those days, I sensed an extra measure of joy and serenity in Joy as we met together—characteristics I wished my own life displayed more. But I was at a much more turbulent place in my life—a place of personal struggle of wanting to do everything well and to find my 'shape' as a woman in ministry. Alongside that, I wanted the church I loved to reach out in the power of God's Spirit and move forward to be all God intended us to be. I was striving hard in so many areas and knew I needed to reach that place of rest I saw in Joy.

A further complicating factor for me was that my own husband, while supportive of my being at college and proud of how well I was doing, was not only a lecturer at college, but also an elder at our church. Along with the rest of the leadership, he had had to work through the question of women elders, which on occasions had made for interesting discussions in our home. At the same time, I was stretching my wings and growing in confidence as a woman in ministry. I believed God had called me to college, yet despite the opportunities I and other women were being given, I felt we were still often 'treated kindly but not taken seriously', as one male conference speaker I heard at the time put it. So the battles raged on, within me and without.

During one visit, I shared with Joy a picture I believed God had given me one evening at church as some of us were praying.

'I saw this old-fashioned circus cage with thick, black bars all around, mounted on a trailer,' I told her. 'Inside, a beautiful, big tiger was prowling up and down, up and down. The cage was too small and the tiger was becoming very agitated. Then, with a mighty crash, the door of the cage was flung open—and in a flash, the tiger had taken off!'

'And what do you think God was saying to you in this picture?' Joy asked.

'Well ... a friend of mine felt I was that tiger and that the picture meant the men of our church were holding me back.'

Joy was silent for a moment, then took a deep breath and sat up straight.

'No!' she said emphatically. 'You are keeping *yourself* in that cage!'

As soon as the words left her mouth, she seemed a little shocked.

'Maybe I shouldn't have said that ...' she exclaimed, putting her hand over her mouth.

For a moment I sat stunned. Joy was never forceful in her opinions—all the more reason, I realised, to take note and to believe God had prompted her to say what she had. And even though I did not like her comment at first, I knew she loved and respected me enough to want the best for me. Joy believed in me—I was aware of that even then. She believed God had called me to college and given me gifts for ministry and, I sensed, would try her utmost to enable me to do what God had for me to do.

Even from her early days as a minister's wife, Joy had resisted conforming to the 'stereotype' of women in that role and tried to discover what she herself was called and gifted to do. And over the years, she had continued to develop her own gifts and ministry alongside David. Then, towards the end of their time at Malabar, Joy had found a ministry of her own developing, as people wanted to talk with her more and more. This led to her undertaking a counselling program and also a course in spiritual direction run by the Catholic Church.

Joy also soon found herself in demand to help run Camp Farthest Out weekends while David remained at home. And from time to time she was now called on to visit other Christian communities like their own as an 'outside visitor' to provide guidance and advice. David was supportive of these ministries that were uniquely Joy's and recognised their importance. He felt that Joy's own ministry should not be kept in the background, especially since he had had the opportunity to minister for around forty years in a public way. And as the years passed, Joy was to run many 'quiet days' and retreats involving art, drama and dance at their home in the mountains.

By the time I met Joy, she firmly supported women developing their gifts to the full and being able to minister in the church and outside it. So while I much preferred to shift the blame for my frustration in this regard off myself and onto the men at church, I knew deep down her comment about my tiger picture was true. She had walked a similar journey and was not going to let me off so lightly—and neither was God.

'It's fine,' I said in the end, trying to smile. 'I'm sure that was important for me to hear. And please keep challenging me when I need to be challenged. I know you have my best interests at heart and that you always listen to God.'

'Well, I try to anyway,' Joy smiled back, still a little apologetic. 'I think we owe it to those with whom we meet to listen both to them and to God. It's almost like having our ears tuned to two different "frequencies" at once.'

'I hope I can do that as well as you do some day, Joy,' I told her. 'I need to go home and reflect more about what you said. I know there are so many things inside me that hold me back.'

However, I was a little too tired, even at that early stage of the year, to do the honest, internal work I needed to do. And while I knew how important it was to think through all the issues surrounding women in ministry, I did not have the time or the energy to tackle it. Yet already I could see what a treasure God had given me in Joy, who believed so passionately in the ability of women to minister, even in ways often regarded as being for men only. Joy had not said what she had about my tiger picture out of disbelief that the men could hold me back—far from it. She knew from her own experience this could well happen. And when on later occasions I saw the depth of her desire to see women fulfilling roles God had called and gifted them to do, I realised afresh how faithful she had been to confront me that day. She could have agreed with my perspective, but instead, with true integrity, chose to alert me to my own personal issues hindering me from moving forward.

And with great wisdom and patience and much prayer on my behalf, she waited for the right time in our relationship to deal with these matters further.

I loved Joy's sensitivity to the work of the Holy Spirit in us and that she believed God could speak directly through spoken words or dreams or pictures, as well as through the written Word. I discovered later how Joy had become more open to these things through the Camp Farthest Out movement and also the teachings of Agnes Sanford and leaders of the charismatic movement in the seventies such as Michael Harper. And eventually, this increased awareness of the gifts of the Spirit had led to both David and Joy's involvement in the healing ministry in Sydney, alongside men such as Canon Jim Glennon.

During another visit to Joy around that time, I shared something that had happened during a recent Sunday morning service.

'I believe God wanted to give me some words of encouragement to pass onto our church, but I couldn't hear them clearly,' I confessed. 'I felt so tired—and also I knew I hadn't been as close to God as I should be. Later that week, I woke up early one morning with that whole event in my mind again. Then I heard God ask me one simple question: *What are you doing to me, Jo-Anne?* I felt so ashamed and convicted—I know I need to do something about how tired I feel. I think I have to make some key decisions about my practical ministry load, but it's a struggle for me to put aside something I said I would do. I hate to inconvenience or disappoint others—and I hate feeling a failure.'

'I think you do need to take note of all this, Jo-Anne,' she said in a gentle but firm way. 'I don't doubt it's a wake-up call from God. You *must* listen to it.'

Already I had learnt that when Joy spoke in this way, I needed to take what she said on board. A few days later, I asked to be released from the role of Pastoral Care Coordinator at our church. And, less than a month after that, I experienced one of my many personal breakthrough times as I again met with Joy.

That day as we talked, I began to cry for no obvious reason, except that I felt so tired. Joy asked if I might be able to have a short break from practical ministry altogether, but I rejected the idea.

'Why would that be so hard?' she asked gently.

'Because ... well, because others at church are just as tired as I am—or even more so. How can I take a break when they can't? Besides, they'd be even busier if I wasn't there,' I argued, trying to mop up my tears.

'Let's focus on you for a moment and forget about them,' Joy continued. 'It seems to me you're very hard on yourself, Jo-Anne. Why is that, I wonder? What's going on inside you right now?'

'I don't know,' I mumbled, unfamiliar with such questions and quite confused.

'What sort of messages is that little voice inside you saying? What are the beliefs driving you?' she persisted. 'Tell me if you can and I'll write them down.'

At first, I was horrified. How could I share such personal thoughts even with Joy, who I knew was so understanding and trustworthy? The struggle was intense—I could not be so honest. After all, my thoughts sounded so childish and petulant. Besides, they might come out all wrong.

I stayed silent. I am sure Joy was praying as she sat opposite, not pressuring me but appearing to expect some sort of response. How faithful she was in not letting me off the hook!

'You know, I can hear one in what you've said already,' she told me, writing it down. '"*If I have my needs met, then I'm being selfish.*" Is that what you feel?'

'Oh yes—that's right,' I agreed, thankful she had covered the awkward moment for me and started the ball rolling. 'Others' needs are much more important than mine.'

'Let's add that then,' Joy said. 'Now what else?'

'Well … perhaps that people won't think well of me if I don't do what they expect,' I muttered, shamefaced. 'I hate disappointing people—I hate anyone to think badly of me.'

Joy wrote these down, then waited for more.

'And I suppose I'd say I like to put myself down first before anyone else does!' I laughed, yet even to my ears, my laugh had a hollow ring.

Joy waited again.

'This all sounds so stupid and childish!' I burst out then.

'Let's write that down too!' Joy smiled.

We both laughed—and I began to realise how refreshing it had been to put those childish beliefs out there for Joy to write down. Yet, in the midst of my laughter, the tears were still there.

We sat in silence a little longer. Then Joy put down her pen and paper and sighed.

'I think you can see how strong these messages are inside you— and they've been there for so long. These things so often become core beliefs that we just accept. We may not know where they come from, but God does. And God can change these negative messages we so often feed on.'

Joy came to stand beside me, laid her hands on my head and began to pray. She did not use many words—they seemed unnecessary. But God was so close to us and very much at work in me as she prayed. Then she led me in a brief exercise where I saw myself sinking back in a comfortable seat and relaxing in Jesus' love for me—it was such a safe place to be. I knew Joy did not expect any response, but after a while, I felt I had to share what God seemed to be doing in me.

'I think I've made one of those core beliefs into a kind of promise to myself, Joy,' I told her. 'I vowed a long time ago I would always make people think well of me. Even as a child, I would be devastated if I ever got into trouble from my parents, let alone anyone else.'

'Let's pray then,' Joy suggested. 'You can ask God to break the power of that vow and let it go, so it doesn't have any control over your life.'

It was such a relief to pray what was on my heart and know God had heard me. I knew even then that while it would take time before my old patterns of behaviour disappeared, I had nevertheless taken an important step in dealing with my lack of self-worth. My time with Joy that morning had given me a glimpse of how powerful and destructive these beliefs were—and I did not want them to control me any longer. Instead, I wanted God to re-mould my beliefs about myself and hold me close in that loving place where I was totally accepted and valued just the way I had been created. From there, I knew I could move out in strength and not resist having my needs met, as I so often did. I was valuable to God. And I needed to take care of myself in the way God wanted me to.

As on many other occasions, Joy searched her bookshelves for something suitable for me to take home and reflect on further.

'Are you familiar with the writings of Henri Nouwen?' she asked me. 'I think you might enjoy some of his work. There's a story he relates in this little book, Out of Solitude.[3] It's about a beautiful, old tree and the fact that its only real use was to provide shade where people could relax and be refreshed. The worth and usefulness of that tree were two different things—that's so important for us to realise, don't you think?'

I drove home that day in a thoughtful mood. So much of my life had been driven by what others would think if I were to fail or displease them. So much of my personal worth had been, and still was, wrapped up in how productive or useful I was being, either by my own standards or those of others. I wanted to live more freely, functioning from that place of complete rest in God's love and acceptance. But I knew there would be challenges ahead. And I knew I would need Joy's support to ensure I didn't fall back into my old patterns of thinking and acting.

Joy continued to be there for me in the following weeks, helping me deal further with the self-doubt that still held me back so much at times, particularly in using my gifts to the full at our church. On the whole, our church was so encouraging to me and supportive of my decision to study at college. I knew I was loved and trusted by so many of our people. Yet some of the difficulties of the past year concerning the exercising of the prophetic gift, intercessory prayer and also women's role in leadership had left their mark. Now I was reluctant to be seen as 'rocking the boat' in any way. I had become wary of sharing prophetic words with our leaders that could be construed as manipulative or as putting forward my own views. I did not want to be misunderstood or regarded as someone with a spiritual axe to grind. During the period when our church leaders were working through the issue of women elders, a leader I respected had said to me: 'Make sure all this isn't just a push for power, Jo.' That comment had stuck—and it hurt.

'I know things like that tap into my self-doubt and that I tend to take them far too personally,' I fumed to Joy one day. 'But who wants to be seen as a pushy, power-hungry female? It's not true at all—I merely believe women God has gifted in leadership should be exercising that gift. Anyway, why is it a different matter if a man seeks to be considered for eldership? Why is that not seen as a push for power too?'

It was wonderful to talk things over with someone who understood such issues and empathised so readily. But it was even more wonderful to experience Joy's ongoing understanding of what was happening for me on a personal level and her openness to the healing and insights the Holy Spirit could bring. On one occasion, I told Joy about the spiritual battle I sensed happening inside me and the accusations I heard in my mind as I walked around praying for people in the area near our church. *This is useless—how will it help anyone? ... You're hopeless. Why don't you go and talk to someone—not just pray! ... You're weak and gutless. You're only doing this because you feel you have to.*

As I shared these things, I also told her about a picture I saw in my mind of the person saying these things. She was a horrible, old woman with wispy hair who accused me in a sneering, derisive voice as she pointed her finger straight at me. Joy suggested I answer her back, which I found so difficult to do. Then, as we talked more about it and prayed, the picture changed to that of a frightened, insecure, little girl with her thumb in her mouth. Jesus came then, picked the little girl up and sat her on his lap, where she seemed to feel very secure. He hugged her and they proceeded to play together, with the little girl even pulling his beard and teasing him. I could feel their happiness at being in each other's company—which in itself was so healing to me.

'You're very good at self-accusation, aren't you?' Joy commented, when we had finished praying and were enjoying the quietness together.

I knew she was right. I was my own worst enemy, constantly feeding that 'inner critic' of mine, yet I did not understand why. At fifteen, I had been overwhelmed for the first time with God's love for me and the fact that I *mattered* to the God of the universe. From that point on, my life direction changed and I committed myself to serve God. Years later, as a busy young mum, God had again broken into my life and reassured me I was a precious child of the King. Then only a few years before meeting Joy, God once again touched my heart and rejuvenated my faith one evening, ministering such accepting love and grace to me. In my mind, I had seen a picture of Jesus holding me as a baby, gazing at me with such love and exclaiming 'Wow—Jo-Anne!' I knew Jesus was showing me he loved me just as he had created me and before I could achieve anything in my life. Yet here I was, still accusing and doubting myself, for some strange reason.

'I don't want to be,' I told Joy then. 'I know I'm totally accepted, just like that little girl on Jesus' lap.'

'Yes, you are—and so am I too,' she replied. 'We can all be as at home with the Lord as that little girl. When you were a child, did you ever lie on a big piece of paper and have someone draw around your shape with a pencil or crayon? That's what I believe the Lord does for each of us. He's the one who draws our shape and 'defines' us. He tells us who we are.'

I loved that simple image. It remained with me in the days and weeks ahead as the year drew to a close and on into my final year at college.

Chapter Four

Finding My Place

In the new year, I took up an invitation to enrol in a mentor training course, along with one other woman and eight men. I so much valued Joy's input into my life that I wanted to be able to help others in a similar manner, particularly potential women leaders. From the outset, I could see that the style of mentoring taught in this course was more structured and goal-oriented and thus quite different from the way Joy and I approached our times together. Yet there were things in common too, in that our trainer stressed the importance of the relational aspect and of mutual respect and commitment to the process.

I felt privileged to be invited to take part in this course, which at the outset involved spending several days away together as a group. Despite my still being a college student, the men in that group treated me kindly but also took me seriously, affirming and respecting me in a way I found very healing. One gifted young man wrote the following words to me at one stage: *Know you have my full support as a man in ministry according to the gifts and call God has given you!* Another wrote how privileged he would feel to serve on any pastoral team with me. Yet I was still so unsure of myself as a woman training for ministry. In one exercise we were asked to complete, we were each given a copy of a meditation called 'The Seed' and asked to reflect on it. This included writing a prayer about our own 'seed' and sharing it with another group member. I was paired with a young man about half my age, which daunted me a little. But the feelings inside me about my 'seed' were so strong, I blurted out my prayer to him anyway:

Lord, I'm afraid it will be crushed. I'm afraid it will never see the light of day. Lord, I'm tired—and maybe my seed is too old to burst into new life. Lord, I need to know you have built a hedge around my seed—it needs all the help it can get to grow. I am so afraid someone will step on it and crush it and grind it into the dirt and break the new little fronds that are beginning to sprout. Lord, I feel very fragile—I feel as if the big heel of a man's heavy boot is crushing the life out of me. Please strengthen me as I confront this fear of being crushed. I know it is from Satan and that he has been defeated—I know you won the victory at the cross.

How wonderful it was to have that young man respond with tears to what I shared! Later, during a public affirmation time, I was equally moved when he in turn took a risk and spoke with such sincerity to me.

'I affirm your voice,' he stated with deep emotion. 'It deserves to be heard.'

Joy delighted in hearing all about the mentor training course. She continued to believe in me and seemed to see what I could not—that I was quite able to stand tall as a woman in ministry and use my gifts to bless others in the unique way I had been created to do. And from what I passed on to her in our many conversations about my ministry roles in our church, she also saw some things I could not see concerning my relationships with the men on our pastoral team.

I was in a strange, unique position in that regard. My husband, while on the staff of our college at the time, was also part of our pastoral team for one day a week. He did not tell me everything he was dealing with in his ministry—far from it. But I could always sense when he was feeling overwhelmed or worried about things. Added to that, the two other men on our team each fulfilled a supervisory role for me in my college studies which required my meeting with them on a regular basis. One was responsible for overseeing my practical ministry and processing any issues involved. And the other helped me reflect on my studies and integrate what I was learning into my life and ministry.

As a result, I spent many hours discussing issues with them both. I respected each of them and was so grateful to them for giving up their time to supervise me. They were in authority over me—yet at times, either intentionally or unintentionally, they would share from their hearts, friend to friend, about issues facing them as pastors and us as a church. On other occasions, while they did not stray from the topic of my studies or ministry responsibilities, I was able to sense if they were burdened about things. As the year progressed, this began to revolve around how the ministry team could best function together and move forward, and soon it emerged that each was questioning his future at our church. Added to that, my husband's role at college was in doubt because of financial issues and changes in course structures.

'I feel sorry for all three men on our team,' I told Joy at one stage. 'There seems to be so much turmoil in their lives right now. I'm sure they don't mean it to happen, but sometimes I'm left feeling very burdened for them in it all. I'm happy to pray for them, but I have enough on my plate without taking on *their* issues as well!'

Joy saw how confused I felt. These men were in leadership roles, yet they were my friends—and one was my husband. I cared about their turmoil, but I was not in a position to provide any solutions, nor did I have the emotional resources to do so. Joy then came up with an unusual idea from my perspective. She asked me to draw how I saw the situation—to map out where I stood in relation to each of these men and how I felt about being there. At first I resisted—the whole concept felt strange to me. But I trusted Joy and respected her wisdom, so did as she asked.

I drew the men in different colours, each colour with its own significance, and placed them at various angles and distances from where I was positioned in the middle.

'As you look at this picture now, is there anything you'd like to change?' Joy enquired.

I found myself tracing a wiggly line from each of them back to me. And even as I drew these lines, I began to feel more distanced from these men and their concerns.

'What are those wiggly lines?' Joy asked me.

'They're meant to be balloon strings,' I laughed, embarrassed not only at my drawing but the thoughts I was expressing. 'I guess I'm saying I'd like them to float away and fight their own battles!'

Joy was silent for a while.

'They look a bit like umbilical cords to me,' she told me then. 'Do you think they might be looking to you for some mothering?'

I was shocked. I did not see it that way, but having experienced Joy's insights on previous occasions, I filed her comment away in my head for further thought.

'Well ... I don't think so,' I responded. 'But I *would* like to be less emotionally involved in it all.'

At that stage in my journey, I also still found myself in awe of the men, with a somewhat unrealistic view of them. They thought and acted differently from me in so many ways. They were much more logical and strategic. And they knew so much more about ministry and theology and church leadership than I did. Somewhere along the line I had made a key judgement—and that was that my way of doing ministry must be inferior and less acceptable than the men's. It was engraved in my spirit—and Joy saw that.

Not long after, it was announced that our two fulltime pastors would be leaving at the end of the year. And around that time, one broached the idea with me that I could join the team after he left. To his surprise, I responded with a very definite 'No, no, no!'—despite my believing that was what God had in mind for me. During a personal retreat time around three years earlier, I felt God had shown me I would be part of our church's ministry team one day and that I was to start getting ready then and there. Yet I had felt so presumptuous, writing such thoughts in my journal. At that time, our church had four wonderful men on our ministry team and as far as I knew, none of them was leaving. Besides, I could not imagine our church's *ever* employing a woman as part of the ministry team—let alone *me*! Now, however, I felt so confused and ambivalent about it all but could not explain why, even to Joy.

'I don't know,' I told her. 'It depends so much on who else is on the team—and in particular, who is the senior pastor. I would have to fit in with their way of doing things—and I don't know if I could do that.'

Joy drew herself up to her full height then.

'Jo-Anne, *they* might need to fit in with *you*, rather than you fit in with them! I believe the Lord wants you to hear that. And don't forget that picture of the tiger in the cage! It's such a female response, don't you think, to be worried about how we will fit in with what the men want to do? You can be strong like that tiger—you have a lot to offer as well.'

Again, however, this was an almost shocking concept to me that the men might need to accommodate *me*. I could not think or act so assertively. I knew God had called me into ministry just the same as the men—yet I still had some distance to travel before I took firm hold of that call.

Only a matter of days after, my husband was retrenched from our college. And soon it became clear our elders envisaged having both my husband and me on our church staff, with my husband becoming fulltime and me being employed part-time. For several reasons, this made me even more confused and ambivalent about taking up such a position. Chief among them was that I was unsure how such an arrangement would affect our marriage. I believed it would be wiser for each of us to have our own space, rather than living and working together. I knew several couples who seemed to function well as a team in ministry yet doubted such an arrangement was wise for us. I felt terrible expressing this opinion—especially since I believed I was in fact called to our church. I could see my hesitation was hurtful to my husband and confusing for some of our elders as well.

Joy listened to me patiently throughout the whole process. She felt my pain and understood my reasons for being wary of such an arrangement but resisted influencing my decision. I admired her for that and valued her prayerful support in this time when I did not even know my own mind. At last, after much thought and prayer, I felt the Lord said, *I'm not asking you to do that just now.* So with a heavy heart, I turned down the invitation to join our pastoral team.

Around three months later, with my husband on long service leave after having left the college staff, we decided to travel to the USA to attend a conference and visit a friend. By that point, I had thought much more about the role of women in both marriage and ministry in an excellent subject, 'Biblical Perspectives on Women', at college. Joy and I had many lively conversations as she shared some of her experiences in ministering alongside David and also leading retreats in her own right. Together we discussed the various biblical passages pertaining to this topic and also other material. At one stage, she shared with me a poem she had written based on the story of the Samaritan woman at the well, which I felt beautifully portrayed Jesus' complete acceptance of this woman and his preparedness to cross cultural and religious barriers to reach out to her:

> *You ask a drink of me*
> *of me, a woman*
> *I see your face reflected*
> *in the water next to mine*
> *And quickly rise to stammer*
> *words of greeting*
> *shot through with surprise*
> *And then you ask a drink of me*
> *and words fall back inside my throat*
> *A stunning thought appears*

that you want gift from me
my company, my waiting on your needs
What could you want of me
Creator of the Universe?
And back the image comes
of your face next to mine
reflected in that water
A look of trusting in your eyes
of joy and pleasure as I take
this day an offering of love
to quench your thirst and mine

I believed Jesus had also reached out to me in a powerful way in my life and I wanted to serve him wherever he called me. But I was still unsure where that might be. At one stage as we prepared to leave for the USA, I sensed God reassuring me that one day I would be part of our church's ministry team, but also warning me I would soon be challenged again about that.

Then late one evening as I sat in the huge, darkened auditorium at the conference in Kansas City after many of the other attendees had left, I knew that moment of challenge had arrived. But the realisation did not fill me with joy at that point. In fact, I sat crying for quite some time at the difficulties ahead and the huge responsibility I would be undertaking. At that moment, two friends from our church back in Australia saw me and asked what was happening. I turned to them with a tearstained face and said: 'I think God wants me to be on the ministry team of our church after all.' After they had prayed with me, I continued sitting in the darkened auditorium as the worship team played and sang words from God over those of us remaining. God's comfort strengthened and filled me—and I knew that whatever happened, I would not be left to fight my battles alone.

But was it too late as far as our church was concerned? Did the offer still stand? When we returned, I wrote to our elders and endeavoured to explain how I had not merely changed my mind. Rather, I was attempting to be obedient to God and do what I was now being called to do. In the end, I was again offered a part-time ministry role on our team. I now knew where I was heading and threw myself into the final months of my studies, eager to be as equipped as possible for what lay ahead.

Through all this turbulent period of indecision, Joy was there for me—a 'safe' person who could listen with objectivity and not be offended by anything I might say. In reality, I believe she kept me afloat in my college years in many ways—so much so that I began referring to her as my 'lifesaver'.

'I don't know how you put up with all my uncertainties and questions about ministry and about myself, Joy,' I said to her on several occasions. 'You must feel so exhausted by the time I leave!'

Joy would smile and tell me yet again what a privilege it was to accompany me on my journey of finding my place in ministry.

'Besides, after you leave, I close the "folder" on all we've talked about and hand it over to God,' she explained, demonstrating with a sweep of her arms how she did.

I remembered that principle often in the years ahead as I prayed with many people tackling difficulties in their lives. I could not take their burdens upon myself—I would sink beneath their weight. But I could close that folder and hand it over to God, praying for grace and strength and healing for them and for the way forward to become clear.

As my college graduation approached, I invited Joy and David to come and to attend the dinner beforehand as my special guests. To my delight, they accepted, despite having to drive down from the mountains. Joy had not been feeling well and later discovered she had whooping cough, but was determined to be there. It was an amazing experience to introduce her to my family and other friends who had supported me all through college. They had heard so much about her and were delighted to meet this one who had played such an important role in my spiritual growth.

But the most fulfilling part of the evening for me was sharing the honour of delivering a speech on behalf of the graduands with a male student who had been appointed as the new senior pastor at our church. Our task was to acknowledge all those who had helped us during our college years and share a little of our own experiences. I was very nervous, so was pleased when my co-speaker suggested we pray together, which calmed us both. I knew this was the moment when I could publicly thank people like Joy who had supported me so much and was looking forward to it. But I felt this was also an opportunity to speak on behalf of other women in ministry and encourage the use of their gifts to the full.

When the time came for me to speak, much to Joy's embarrassment, I included the following:

> *I would like to thank our practical ministry supervisors, our integration supervisors and also our spiritual mentors for the many hours they have expended in coming alongside us, helping us understand issues, sharing their expertise and their lives with us. I call my spiritual mentor my 'lifesaver' because that is what she truly has been for me.*

Later, I also mentioned what a wonderful gift my time at college had proved to be—something I had wanted to do for so long. I shared how valuable and holistic my training had been and how God had stretched me in every way. But I also wanted to make the point that academic learning and grasping the 'how to' of ministry were only part of the picture. Joy had helped me see how important it also was to grow in knowing God and not merely knowing *about* God. And as I expressed it that evening, I was so glad she and others had rescued me from graduating with a head crammed full of knowledge and skills but with a heart dead to the things of the Spirit.

I was also able to mention something of my journey as far as being a woman in ministry was concerned. I did not mention Joy by name, but every word I said was spoken with her in mind.

> *Finally, my time at college has helped me see I do have a place as a woman in ministry, with unique gifts to be used to build up the body, and has strengthened and challenged*

*me to take up the responsibility of the leadership role God
has given me.*

As I finished that sentence, some of the pastors and leaders from our church cheered out loud. I looked towards where they were seated and saw Joy beaming too. And I suspect she was also part of the group of supporters who blew party whistles and clapped loudly as I made my way to the platform to receive my diploma from our college principal. This time, it was *my* turn to be embarrassed! Yet I was also very touched by the joy they expressed on my behalf.

To my surprise, I also received two awards, including dux of our year. It was wonderful to share that moment with Joy and to see how proud and pleased she was for me. That evening, she gave me a card on which she had written:

Dear Jo
I was remembering the picture of the caged tiger tonight!
Very special to be here with you. Grace and peace and love
Joy—from your cheering squad!

I did not want our relationship to end. I knew I would need Joy's input and loving support just as much, if not more, as I began my part-time ministry role at our church. With some trepidation, I asked her if she would consider meeting with me on an ongoing basis.

'Of course—I'd be delighted!' she responded. 'That's if you still feel it's worth taking the time to drive up here.'

I felt I would not be able to manage seeing her more often than once a month, but was determined to stick to that arrangement, whatever else I had to forego. Apart from benefiting from her support and prayer, I knew I had so much more to glean from her in areas such as listening to God, different forms of prayer and meditation, and self-care. Joy had ministered in so many different and deep ways to people over the years, albeit often in an unsung and unofficial role, and I knew had much to offer in enabling me to become the pastor God had called me to be. I was to serve on a team with three men, one being my husband—and somehow I had to find my own unique way of ministering in the midst of it all.

CHAPTER FIVE

EMBRACING MINISTRY

Two weeks before my college graduation, I had been inducted ahead of time into ministry at our church. I had requested our then senior pastor, who had supported me throughout my time at college as my integration supervisor and who had always believed in me as a woman in ministry, to perform this simple but profound ceremony before he left. And I had wanted the associate minister, who was also leaving and who had supervised my practical ministry, to pray for me as I was inducted. I was delighted when both agreed.

The induction took place during our normal Sunday morning service, which Joy unfortunately could not attend. This was the moment when our church members agreed to support me as a pastor and when I committed myself to serving God and them. In his initial comments, our senior pastor congratulated me on being voted in overwhelmingly to serve on our ministry team, but reminded me that this brought with it significant responsibility. Our church members trusted me, along with the other pastors, to set direction and lead well, providing a

Christlike example in every way. But he also reminded me I would have limited personal capacity to do this and would need to draw constantly on God for strength and wisdom. The formal charge to serve as a pastor was then put to me:

> *In spite of the huge challenges ahead, but in view of God's grace to you, will you accept this call to be a pastor of this church?*

After I had responded, the church was reminded that each one of them was now called to encourage, respect and honour me in my ministry. And as they stood to affirm their support, I experienced an overwhelming sense of God's faithfulness and grace. I was now part of our church's ministry team, just as God had told me I would be prior to going to college. It had taken five years to become a reality—five years during which I had often doubted it would ever happen. Yet, despite my lack of faith, God had brought it about.

Then our associate pastor prayed a beautiful prayer on my behalf. Among other things, he prayed the church would welcome me into their hearts as their pastor and that I would take on only the 'yoke' that God was placing on me. He asked God for a new joy in my heart, for a fresh passion in ministry and also for my gifting to be taken to a new level.

Buoyed by this wonderful support from the men of our old pastoral team and by the whole church, I embarked on my first official term of ministry. I knew a small minority were ambivalent about having a woman as part of the ministry team, yet I still valued them as people and respected their right to hold a different view. And they were well and truly outnumbered by those who supported me, for which I was thankful. I did not take lightly the fact that people who had known me for years had now put their trust in me in a new and deeper way—and I was determined to honour and serve both God and them with all my heart.

From the beginning, it was obvious I needed to be much more realistic about what I could achieve in two days of ministry each week. My husband and I had both decided we would work an extra day unpaid, since many other committed church members spent hours each week involved in ministry. But even with three days at my disposal, how was I to manage all the things I felt called to do?

It took weeks of discussion for our team to find the best way to function together and use our gifts well. Our new senior pastor, a gifted man in his early thirties, had been appointed to lead us. My husband, then in his late fifties, had been employed in an interim fulltime capacity to provide an important link between our old ministry team and the new. And the third male team member, a young man in his late twenties, was employed part-time to work with our evening congregation and oversee our youth program. These three men were all very different, with differing degrees of ministry experience. And then there was I, new to a formal ministry role, yet also experienced in many areas.

I wanted to do so much. Even before heading to college, I had been involved in a range of ministries at our church, particularly in the areas of music and prayer. During college, my practical ministry roles had included oversight of pastoral care, worship leading, prayer counselling, staff devotions in our child care centre, intercession, and missions involvement, plus some mentoring of younger Christians. Now we had to work out where God wanted me to focus my attention.

We all saw the need to train others to take on more leadership responsibility rather than doing everything ourselves, but for me, this seemed easier said than done. I tended to see a need and want to do something about it myself. And I also found it hard to ask others to do things, in case I was imposing on them. I still needed Joy's wisdom to help me pinpoint what personal issues within me were driving such behaviour.

And she did not let me down. It was always a special treat to put ministry aside for a while, take that beautiful drive up the mountains again and talk through things with her. I was well aware by then of her desire to create a safe place for others and to be present with them in every way. Sometimes her listening, caring presence was all I needed—a wonderful gift to a busy pastor. But usually Joy asked gentle questions, reflecting what she heard and observed, suggesting useful resources and, on occasions, sharing her own thoughts on the way forward. She also rejoiced in the positive things happening in my ministry and was always delighted when I shared some way God had worked amongst us.

'I hope all this doesn't bore you,' I would say to her at times. 'It's not your church and you don't know any of the people I've mentioned.'

'It's a privilege to hear about it all,' she would always respond. 'It's like I'm ministering vicariously along with you!'

Joy meant it too. For her, it brought to mind some of the many unique and diverse ministries in which she herself had been involved over the years—a young wives' group at Miranda, caring for several unmarried mothers-to-be at Bondi and treating them as part of the family, using creative movement in worship, involvement in the healing ministry and the Order of St Luke, playgroups at Malabar, and a Christian Dance Fellowship group, to name a few. Then, along with David and others, Joy had played a vital role in setting up their 'common purse' community as part of the Malabar church, inspired by the Community of Celebration in Houston, Texas. Both she and David were also involved in 'The Fisherfolk' music ministry in the seventies and began introducing new ways of worshipping God through music, song, liturgical dance and art. Also, with the Malabar church's concern for local issues, Joy was active in neighbourhood ministries, particularly to the marginalised—children's holiday programs, 'resale' shops, a food co-op, creative efforts such as painting a huge mural with the local people, and even running a post office and gift shop. As well, working with Peninsula Community Services, the 'common purse' community ran a local newspaper and retrained unemployed people.

It was while still at Malabar that Joy began to find herself more and more in demand, not only to lead workshops in creative worship, writing, drawing and prayer for Camp Farthest Out, but also as a counsellor and spiritual companion. After David and Joy bought their property in the Blue Mountains, she also led many creative retreats and 'quiet afternoons' there. And in David's final placement at Surry

Hills, Joy was again involved in ministry to the marginalised, often taking up social justice issues on their behalf. It was at this point that she met up with Marnie Kennedy, a Catholic nun who became her great friend and spiritual companion and with whom she went on to lead 'street retreats'. These retreats sent out groups who walked the inner city streets or sat wherever people congregated. Their aim was to be present in a prayerful way, letting God speak through what they experienced. While at Surry Hills, Joy also completed a thirty day Ignatian retreat[4] and an Elijah House prayer ministry course[5], using the insights gained to good effect in her counselling and spiritual direction work.

With all this ministry experience and training, both formal and informal, Joy was easily able to relate to my ministry challenges. She loved to see the freedom I had as a woman to step into all sorts of roles in our church and undertake new ventures. More and more, I was being asked to preach in our morning service, and on occasions, I would run by her what I felt I needed to say in an upcoming sermon.

'Oh, that's *wonderful*, Jo-Anne!' she would sometimes exclaim, not so much referring to what I intended to say, but more to the fact that I was able to speak so freely to both men and women.

Joy's responses were a good reminder not to take the privilege of my paid ministry position for granted. I was indeed so grateful for the opportunity God had given me and did not want to waste my energies on things I was not meant to be doing. But what was I to give up? Even after some months, I still found it difficult to formulate any succinct job description, while our senior pastor had too much on his hands at first to think about such things. And when we did discuss it, we could not reach any clear agreement on the subject.

I loved preaching and wanted to do more. I enjoyed worship leading, which involved choosing songs and organising the flow of our morning service. I was very much at home in intercession and in prayer ministry with individual people. I was growing more in the gift of prophecy and was trusted by the leaders to pass on anything I believed God was saying to our church, as well as train others in this area. I was mentoring several young women one-on-one, all with leadership potential. I believed this was the most strategic means of raising up leaders, and while it was time consuming, I was convinced it was worth it. I enjoyed taking devotions for both our child care centre and family support staff. I was part of our missions committee and was passionate about supporting our workers overseas. I was becoming excited about the recovery groups we planned to run and undertook training to lead these. And of course there were pastoral visits, occasional weddings, funerals and baby dedications, elders' meetings, planning meetings and church social events as well. Also, I sometimes took on speaking events outside our church, such as women's camps and Walk to Emmaus weekends.

I was over-committed, but felt driven to do it all. In part at least, this stemmed from the fact that I was now seeing firsthand how much women could contribute in ministry. Some women found it easier to talk with another woman about issues in their lives, however gentle and approachable our male pastors were. And, as far as preaching was concerned, I was aware that some in our congregation, both men and women, appreciated my more 'feminine' approach to topics at times and my general way of speaking. Two men in particular, who I knew did not even believe women should preach, would go out of their way to thank me whenever I spoke and affirm me for the strong biblical message I had shared.

I also knew that no one else could lead our first recovery group for women and train others in this. And I could not see how others could mentor my 'girls', whom I regarded as potential leaders. It took time to build such trusting relationships, just as it had in my own experience with Joy, and I valued the rapport I enjoyed with these young women. One was soon to head overseas as a missionary and I wanted to support her as much as I could before she left. Another had prophetic gifts, but was also going through big shifts in her personal life, so I knew she needed loving, sensitive input to maintain her Christian growth. Still another excelled as a gifted musician and worship director, but was almost buckling under the stress of maintaining a high-powered secular job while supporting her husband through college. I could not leave any of them floundering.

Everywhere I looked, I saw so many ministry opportunities. I knew I needed Joy's input to help me step back and see what shape God wanted my ministry to be. And, above all, I needed her loving admonitions to care for myself in the midst of these ministry pressures and preserve my times of quiet alone with God.

'You don't have to talk at all, you know,' she said on more than one occasion when I must have looked tired. 'We can just be quiet and enjoy God together or you can go out to *The Quiet House* and be by yourself, if you prefer. You can even lie down and sleep if that would help. Please do whatever you need to do for yourself.'

Joy modelled so well the concept of hospitality as applied to spiritual direction—that opening up of her own personal space as well as her home. Whenever she welcomed me, I knew she was prepared to give me not only her time and attention but anything else I needed, whether a bed or books or cups of Lady Grey tea. Often too she would share interesting little snippets of wisdom—a line from a poem, some saying gleaned from one of the early Christian contemplatives, perhaps a meditation or a prayer. Sometimes I would scribble these down in my journal to reflect on many times over, until they became part of me too. At other times, Joy would search her shelves to see if she could find the book containing whatever it was she had shared. Then, having found it, she would lend it to me without a second thought or photocopy the relevant page. At times too, in the course of her own reading, she would stumble across a quote she felt might help me and post me a copy. And whenever she did, she always included an encouraging note or a special card. One of the first cards she sent was homemade, with a flower drawn on it and the words '*Loving God means letting God love us*' written below. Inside, I found a quote Joy had seen elsewhere, urging me to attend to those neglected places deep within.

On another occasion, it was a quote from a poem by Swinburne containing the words '*I bid you but be*'[6]—something I always struggled to do. And on yet another, it was some perceptive lines from the poet and artist Michael Leunig, whose writings and cartoons we both enjoyed, about carrying our cross well in this world.[7]

I needed that wisdom and harmony in my life. And I needed it even more when the marriage of one of our children broke down, causing us all much grief and leading me to question what I was doing in ministry. Everything seemed unreal as I listened to our daughter telling us about it one Sunday just after I had preached—how could this have happened under our very noses? I continued on through those weeks, but my heart was heavy and preaching in particular took its toll on my emotions.

Once again, I experienced Joy's loving support and sincere empathy in the midst of it all. She seemed to know intuitively what I needed to hear—or was it that God prompted her? Joy rarely shared personal details about her children with me. I knew she had four daughters, and that she and David enjoyed spending time with them and their families. Sometimes she would tell me little family snippets—news of wonderful, imaginative birthday celebrations or trips away together or different career choices they were making. They all seemed gifted and interesting, with strong views about caring for the earth and alternate education models and different ways of 'doing' church. At times I would have liked to ask Joy more about them, but did not wish to pry into her private life. However, when I shared about our daughter's marriage, after a moment's silence, Joy seemed to come to a decision.

'I can identify with how you must be feeling, Jo-Anne,' she began. 'One of our daughters is separated from her husband—and I can remember how painful that process was for all concerned.'

It was only a simple, brief statement, but it touched me. I had felt such a failure. Here was I, so busy helping others that I had not noticed my own daughter's deep distress. But here was Joy, whose ministry I valued so much, opening her heart and life to me, telling me a similar thing had happened in their family. In a topsy-turvy kind of way, this comforted me so much and reassured me I could move forward through it all—and so could our daughter.

'Thanks, Joy,' I whispered. 'Thanks for telling me that.'

From that point on, I respected Joy even more. She had experienced the same thing. She understood. And she ministered to others with even more empathy as a result.

Joy also seemed to know which books I would enjoy and benefit from reading. Early on in my ministry, she shared with me some of the writings of Teresa of Avila. Not long after, I pinned up one short quotation from this saintly woman where I could see it each day: *Let nothing disturb you. Let nothing frighten you. Everything passes away except God.*[8] In the midst of all my busyness and personal turmoil, these words gave me a much needed focus and reminded me of the bigger picture. Joy also recommended further books by Henri Nouwen, a Dutch Catholic priest and member of the L'Arche community founded by Jean Vanier. Nouwen's own spiritual journey through doubts and struggles, recounted so vulnerably in his book *The Road to Daybreak*,[9] challenged me and fed my spirit. I explored some of the wonderful writings on Celtic spirituality on Joy's shelves and my vision was enlarged in the process. As time permitted, I read some of her beloved, old novels by British Christian author Elizabeth Goudge, including her favourite, *The Scent of Water*.[10] And later, I was to discover Madeleine L'Engle[11] and, like Joy, fall in love with her writings.

But Joy shared more than books with me. During one visit towards the end of that year, she showed me a postcard in blue and gold tones depicting an angel—obviously a fresco on a church wall or ceiling. The angel's arms were held high in a strong and powerful pose.

'This is part of the paintings on the dome of St Paul's Cathedral in London,' she explained. 'I'm convinced this is a female angel—don't you agree? She reminds me of you—she looks so strong and powerful and seems to be so fearlessly declaring a message to the world.'

I laughed but was moved and encouraged all the same.

When I next saw Joy, she handed me a rectangular shaped gift.

'I'm a little disappointed how this came out, but I wanted it to remind you to keep on fighting and being that powerful woman in ministry. I hope you can find a spot for it.'

Inside, I found an enlarged colour photocopy of 'our' angel from St Paul's. Joy had found a blue wooden frame that perfectly matched the blue tones of the painting. I have it to this day on my study wall where it still serves to remind me of the strength God gives me day by day.

I looked for that angel when, just over twelve months later, as the world welcomed in the new millennium, I visited St Paul's Cathedral for the first time. I had been given a free return flight to Europe, courtesy of a friend who wanted me to accompany her to the Netherlands, Germany and Britain. As I made my way across the black and white chequered floor of St Paul's and gazed up into its massive dome, I thought of Joy. And there, high above me, was our angel, I was sure.

I continued on to the small side-chapel where the Holman Hunt painting 'The Light of the World' is located. I sat in silence, contemplating the artist's portrayal of Jesus standing outside the door with his lamp held high, waiting to be invited in. After a while, I did exactly that. I invited him into my life afresh, asking him to empower me for the ministry that lay ahead. Then just as I went to leave, I saw the small figure of a nun standing in the high pulpit in the centre of the cathedral and heard her beautiful, gentle voice leading everyone in prayer. I was amazed—how was it that at that exact moment it happened to be a *woman* calling everyone in the cathedral to prayer? In my heart, I knew God was challenging me yet again to be faithful as a woman in ministry and to embrace the call I had been given.

Chapter Six

Challenges

Meanwhile, as my first year in ministry ended, despite my tiredness, I found myself looking forward to another year on team. But the question as to which ministries I should undertake remained. And I was concerned that, in the midst of my busy life, I seemed to be losing some of my intimacy with God. I decided to schedule in a personal retreat before the year began in earnest. I knew this was what Joy would encourage me to do and felt quite proud of the fact that I was putting into practice a self-care measure she often urged me to employ.

During my retreat, I sensed again God's close, comforting presence, so vital for me in all I was undertaking. I mapped out a weekly schedule for the year ahead, setting aside two days for writing—something I was being drawn to more and more. I felt I wanted to preach at least once a month. I would restrict myself a little in mentoring, I decided, but still meet regularly with at least four young women from our church. I would begin to teach on some aspects of prayer ministry and also continue to schedule in some prayer counselling appointments. I would oversee the two recovery courses being offered in the coming year. I would still lead worship. And I would attend all the various meetings and church events necessary. But I would have to set aside some things I loved, including taking devotions for our child care centre staff and supervising college students.

I was also determined to care for myself better—something else Joy often encouraged me to do.

'What can you do to relax, Jo-Anne?' she would ask. 'Can you drive somewhere and sit and read? Or is there a symphony concert coming up you might enjoy? It's important to be kind to yourself and nurture your soul and spirit.'

This was not something I was used to doing, but as the year progressed, I tried to find time to put all thought of ministry aside and enjoy the moment. And I also tried to recognise what was happening inside me—another skill Joy had encouraged me to develop.

'It's so important to listen to our bodies,' she would tell me. 'After all, we are whole beings, so how we are travelling spiritually and emotionally will be reflected in physical ways in our bodies.'

Again, this was something I had to a large extent ignored. Years earlier, I had decided I needed to forge ahead, whatever was happening inside me—that it was an indulgent luxury to acknowledge any feelings of sadness or exhaustion or frustration. But now I began to see the wisdom of what Joy was saying. And this self-understanding developed further as Joy introduced me to some key resources she herself had found helpful, one of which was a technique called focusing, pioneered by Eugene Gendlin.[12] Focusing involves recognising what is happening in our bodies and becoming aware of that 'felt sense' within, which can often lead to greater insight and healing.

At first, Joy gently took me through my own focusing experience after I arrived one day in a rather tumultuous frame of mind. We sat in silence for a while, each acknowledging God's presence, after which Joy encouraged me to try to become aware of what was happening in my body. Then she began to ask some questions I at first found difficult.

'Can you ask yourself if there's anything in your life right now that's keeping you from feeling good or free?'

I was reluctant to admit, even to myself, some of the family and church issues bothering me. But I could not deny they were there.

'If you find a few issues surfacing, can you sense which one's bothering you the most?' she continued in her gentle voice. 'Take your time—but let me know when you've found it, if you can.'

I searched around as best I could within me. Then with surprising clarity, I recognised the issue causing the greatest concern.

'Yes, it's there,' I whispered.

'Is there some word or image you can associate with this sense that describes it or pictures it well? Can you ask it that?'

At first I thought it all very strange but decided to go along with what was happening. I trusted Joy and I knew God was present.

'Can you ask your body if it's okay to be with this sense inside you? If it is, then just sit with it and befriend it. What does it feel like? ... What does it look like? ... Can you get to know it a bit better?'

I began to see this prickly ball of fear over the issue that had come to me and sense something akin to panic. I sat still, feeling the weight of it and holding it before God.

'Can you ask what this felt sense needs? ... What would make it feel better or more comfortable?'

I knew God was an integral part of this whole process. And I sensed this fear inside me needed to be held by Jesus, close to his heart, until it became much softer and smaller. I handed that prickly ball over and watched as Jesus held it. And just as I had hoped, it soon became softer and smaller. The whole process seemed somewhat bizarre—yet I knew God was working within me, bringing healing and putting things right.

Then Joy continued.

'Now can you check what is happening in your body? Is anything different from when we started?'

I nodded.

'Does it need anything more from us today? ... Is there anything more it wants to tell you?'

I shook my head this time, sensing God had done what was needed for the moment.

'Then can you say a gentle thank you to your body for showing you what it has? And perhaps you can promise to revisit all this again soon, if you feel comfortable with that.'

We waited again in silence for a few moments. I felt so at peace— and amazed that such an unusual and simple process could tell me so much about what was happening inside me. Joy did not pressure me to share what I had experienced but I decided I would like to. Then together we both thanked God—our God who created us as mind, body, soul and spirit, who knows us intimately and who can heal and renew in such unique ways.

During a later visit, Joy guided me through another similar form of this process, and again I could see its great value. It was yet another God-given tool, I believed, to help not only me but others as well. While I had difficulty explaining the process to others, I knew in my heart it worked and that God could bring good out of it.

As the year progressed, I began to suspect I would need every tool God could give me to continue to do ministry well and stay whole. I loved our church so much and I loved and respected the men on our ministry team. I was optimistic about our future as a congregation. There had been many prayers prayed over the years for our church and for the people of 'the valley', as the surrounding area was called. God had given us encouraging prophetic words, we believed, telling us we would soon reap a harvest through our ministries as we remained faithful. Some of us still gathered together each week to worship and pray and hear how God wanted us to reach out to others. As well, our ministry team tried to pray together and ask for God's guidance. Yet despite all this, with a sinking heart, I began to sense difficult days ahead for us as a team.

I had been called onto our ministry team for one year at first and then for three further years, as had my husband. But as time went on, my husband was becoming more and more dissatisfied and restless, sensing his gifts were not being used to their full extent. His main pastoral responsibilities were overseeing our home groups and training up group leaders, as well as regular preaching, but increasingly he was beginning to feel sidelined. He was aware he had been appointed to provide a bridge between the old and new pastoral teams—was his job now done? Was God now calling him elsewhere? And if so, was I to stay at our church or go with him?

As he struggled to ascertain what God was saying, I struggled too. I wanted my husband to be happy and fulfilled in ministry with all my heart. I did not seek to hold him back in any way from what God had for him. But I also became convinced God wanted me to stay on at our church. I wondered too, with a heavy heart, whether my husband had felt a little pushed out by my being on team—whether perhaps this had contributed to his sense of being sidelined. What was I to do in this situation?

To make matters worse, while I supported my husband and was well aware how much I owed him concerning how to go about ministry, I also wanted to support our other team members, particularly our senior pastor. Yet this young man had quite a different philosophy of ministry from my husband and wanted to approach things in his own time and way. He was still growing in his role and I felt we had to allow him space to do that and to 'bumble along', as he himself put it, not knowing at times how he should do things. I loved his prayerful, godly approach to the issues we were confronting. I believed in him and wanted to do as much as I could to help him in his leadership role. One morning around this time, I felt God gave me a picture of this young man trying on a crown in front of a mirror. At first he put it on lopsided and laughed at himself. He continued playing with the crown, trying it on this way and that. At last, feeling so frustrated, I took hold of the crown and pushed it down hard on his head so that it stayed firm. I felt this picture was a challenge from God for him to believe more in himself and his call to lead the church, to put his doubts aside and to wear his leadership crown with pride.

I therefore felt torn—and it became exhausting. But Joy was an invaluable support, listening with great patience to my ramblings and praying for me. She was my 'lifesaver' all over again, just as she had been during my college years.

'Can you take some time off?' she suggested to me around the middle of that year. 'You need to look after yourself. Besides, this may give you a "window" when you can think more clearly about things.'

I took her advice and headed to my sister's home in Brisbane for a week, feeling drained and exhausted. I was also quite confused—nothing seemed clear cut anymore. I wrote in my journal that week: *I feel I'm not really 'here'—that I am a long way off somewhere. How can I recover?*

But God did not leave me in that confused place for long. Towards the end of that week, God reminded me I had been chosen to bear fruit where I had been planted. I was not to walk away from what I had been called to do at our church and, in fact, had a very important part to play.

Encouraged, I returned home, but the battle continued. I needed Joy's listening ear and ongoing advice more than ever—and again she did not let me down. She continued to help me see my worth as a woman in ministry and to believe God had not made a mistake by giving me the gift of leadership, along with teaching, prophecy and encouragement.

'Remember the picture of the caged lion,' she told me more than once. 'And remember that time a lady at your church called you "Joan of Arc". What was it she said to you?'

'She felt God wanted me to know I needed to be leading at the forefront of the battle, like Joan of Arc,' I told her with a sigh.

I was tired and feeling such a weight of responsibility. On another visit to Joy around that time, she asked me if I could draw her two pictures—one depicting where I felt I was now in ministry and one of where I would like to be.

'But I'm a hopeless artist!' I protested.

'That doesn't matter. Sometimes drawing how we're feeling helps make sense of it all.'

I tried my best and soon found myself sketching out quite detailed pictures. In the first, I was positioned upright in a chasm, tears gushing out and arms and legs stretched out and shaking as I tried to anchor myself on each side above a huge drop to the ground below. I labelled the rock face on my right 'church work and demands', while the one on my left I called 'our senior pastor'. Then in that same picture, I also drew the big hand of God reaching down and lifting me clean out of the chasm. In my second picture, the chasm had closed over and I was standing on solid ground. I drew Jesus standing beside me and together we stepped easily across the spot where the chasm had been. We then moved on past several milestones, each bearing the name of one of the ministries I felt called to do at our church.

'That's what I want to be free to do,' I told Joy through my tears. 'Mentoring, outreach to women, recovery groups, prayer ministry training—and, of course, preaching.'

In the middle of these two pictures, I had also drawn a hammock suspended between two trees. I was fast asleep in it as it rocked to and fro. At the time, Joy and I thought this stood for the week's leave I had taken. It was not until months later that I was to understand the full significance of this part of my drawing and realise the milestones could well have been speaking of something quite different.

As my third year of ministry drew to a close, my husband made the decision to leave our church. His job was done—simple as that. We did not know at that point what he would be doing the following year, but he was content to wait for God to show him what was next. He had been in some form of ministry all our married life and knew he could trust God with his future. Meanwhile, I stayed on—and inherited my husband's role of oversight of home groups. I became fulltime on our ministry team—and busier than I had ever been.

In March that year, my mother passed away in Brisbane after a long battle with stomach cancer. I felt guilty I had not been there to care for her or even visit her and that I had left it all up to my sister, but had been unable to spend long periods away from our church. Two years earlier, my father had also passed away in Brisbane. I had flown up then for the funeral and, after being away only a few days, had preached in our morning service. I vowed not to do that again this time. I felt I needed space to grieve and get used to the idea that my parents were no longer around, but there was too much to do in ministry to be idle for long.

Again, Joy understood and warned me yet again to be kind to myself, to listen to my body and to set aside quiet times with God for replenishment. And she also tried to encourage me to say 'no' more often when asked to do ministry tasks I felt I could not manage. Bit by bit, it was becoming clear to me that the role I had inherited from my husband of overseeing our home groups was not a good fit. I was overloaded as it was, but had felt I should take on this task to ensure the structure and training he had put in place would not fall in a heap. I wanted to honour his work in this way—especially since he was still feeling the loss of his ministry role. And I suspect I also wanted to prove to the men I could do whatever I was asked.

I also wondered if I needed to say 'no' more often when given a task too late for it to be done well. This did not seem to affect the men on our team so much, but I was a perfectionist from way back. I needed time to pray and prepare and feel I had something worthwhile to offer. I was happy to handle many things without any notice, such as sharing a prophetic word for our church or praying for someone. But I did not appreciate being asked to do tasks I felt could have been given to me much earlier with a little more forethought.

'Am I just being difficult?' I asked Joy. 'Everyone's busy—and both men on team have young families. Perhaps I should be more accommodating. I think our senior pastor might feel I'm judging him a bit—that he somehow has to live up to my standards.'

I knew I needed to demonstrate as much grace as I could on our team and not be too rigid. After all, I wanted everything to run well for our team and our church as a whole. And I truly wanted our senior pastor to succeed in his leadership role. For these reasons, I talked to Joy about whether the Myers-Briggs Type Indicator assessment tool or some similar personality test might help our team understand one another and our approaches to ministry better.[13]

'I've already suggested this on team, but nothing's happened,' I told her. 'I remember in my mentor training completing a self-perception inventory to find the team role that best described me. I discovered I'm a "completer" or a "finisher"—I don't like leaving jobs half done and get annoyed if people don't carry through on what they say they'll do. And I think I'm a bit of a "shaper" too—I like a clear outcome from a discussion and can be intolerant with vague ideas and people. So I may not be a very comfortable person to work with!'

'But they might well need you on team,' Joy reminded me. 'And we all have strengths and weaknesses. Tell me, have you heard of the Enneagram?'

I hadn't and was curious to find out more.

'It's a very ancient system that centres around what are termed the nine basic personality types,' Joy explained. 'It highlights our strengths and weaknesses, but also shows how we can change and react to things in better ways. I can lend you some books about it, if you like, although it's much better to explore the Enneagram in a workshop context. I remember I thought I was one personality type until I attended one and realised I wasn't.'

I knew I had no time to attend anything at that point, but I read the books with interest. And as I did, I saw in myself strong elements of a Type One personality—that is, the 'achiever' or the 'good person'. I was a perfectionist, according to my personality description, striving to bring order and put things right. I also tended to impose my high standards on others and feel angry and resentful when nothing changed. And I hated it when others wanted to reinvent the wheel and put aside something that was working fine. But there were also some more positive aspects to my personality type, I noted with relief. I prepared well for things ahead of time. I was a kind and gentle leader. I was loyal and had integrity. I was able to recognise reality. And I could inspire others with a belief in themselves. Yet underneath all this was a deep belief that I had to be perfect to be loved.

I related to all these points—particularly the more negative ones. Only a matter of days earlier, I had objected in a team meeting to spending hours writing new training material of our own rather than use something others had written. And I was quite aware I had high standards and strong perfectionist tendencies. But was I also guilty of imposing these high standards on my colleagues? Or was it *their* problem if they felt pressured to measure up? Perhaps it was a mixture of both—I could not tell. But discovering the Enneagram forced me to look at myself and work at changing or 'redeeming' those aspects of my personality that could well lead to team disharmony. And it also gave me a much clearer idea of how others might perceive me.

I was so glad Joy had introduced this valuable tool to me. While it challenged me to be a better person, it also reminded me that God loved me, however perfect or imperfect I was. I remembered again the picture God had given me years earlier of Jesus holding me as a little baby and looking at me with such love and delight. And I also remembered another picture given at the same time of all my academic achievements and certificates being bundled in a blanket and pushed to one side by God's hand, indicating they were not important. What mattered was God's amazing love for me. And I knew I needed to rest in that love and approach the challenges of ministry with confidence from that place of deep love and security.

Chapter Seven

Further Challenges

Soon after that, it was time to consider my own future at our church. After some discussion, I was offered another five year term of ministry. I prayed long and hard about this. On one hand, I loved our church and did not want to leave—I felt God still had many things to do through me there. But, on the other hand, I was very tired. And I was also concerned about the ability of those of us on team to work well together. Did we have the right combination of people and gifts on team for our church to function well?

To complicate matters further, my husband had begun an intentional interim ministry at a church in the Blue Mountains. His task was to transition the church from where they were to a point where they would be ready to welcome a new senior pastor. As husband and wife, we had always talked about church matters together. Now, however, we had not one church's issues to discuss, but two! Unless we were careful, it was easy to become even more drained as we tried to support each other.

In the end, I felt I needed to stay on at our church and again my call was confirmed when a large majority of our members voted for me to continue. But, by the end of that year, I began questioning my decision. Our team was still not functioning well from my perspective. This was puzzling and disturbing to me—I hated any discord with a passion. I still loved my colleagues and wanted all of us to reach our full potential in ministry, but something was wrong. While my inability to clarify my ministry roles was causing great frustration on our team, I felt equally frustrated by what I perceived as a lack of clear leadership and other related issues. In this situation, it was hard for any of us to focus on our ministry tasks.

In mid-December, while trying yet again to work out my job description, we had the most serious disagreement we had ever had in our team. I was aghast—it was the last thing I wanted. How could it ever have come to this? No doubt our end-of-year tiredness was a contributing factor, but I knew it went far deeper. Feeling disappointed with myself and my responses, but also hurt and confused by some things that had been said, I decided to take a few days' leave. I arranged to stay further up in the mountains from where Joy lived and then visit her later. I wanted to spend time with God by myself first and in the beauty of creation. I hoped this would help me process all that had happened, so I could share things better with Joy.

My first stop was the Leura Cascades—a beautiful, secluded little park with various walks winding through bushland and onto the edge of the escarpment. I followed one path to a lookout and stood gazing down on the valley below and the expanse of tree-covered mountains, stretching as far as the eye could see. Surely God was bigger than the problems on our team? Surely there was a way through our misunderstandings and difficulties?

Too tired to walk further, I returned to a spot where I had seen a secluded seat underneath an overhanging rock. Joy often talked about seeing and hearing God in nature and I knew I needed to experience that. I sat there for a long time, trying to still the turmoil in my mind and drink in the peace and the healing God had for me. My hand rested on the firm rock beside me and I could hear the wind stirring the leaves of the tall trees and water cascading through the nearby undergrowth. From time to time, the tears flowed—I was so glad my solitude was interrupted only occasionally by one or two stray bushwalkers. I was aware of a deep, deep sadness in me and almost a horror at the way things had transpired on our team in recent times.

After a while, I tried to think about it all with more objectivity, but could not. And I sensed God did not expect this of me at that point. I stayed where I was, merely being with God, as Joy had talked about so often, and sensed that loving Presence all around me, comforting and upholding me. I did not want to move, but eventually returned to my car and headed further up the mountains. Later that day, I wrote the following in my journal:

> *Lord, I feel so sad deep inside, but I thank you for the beautiful time this morning, walking at Leura and just sitting and being, surrounded by your creation. I feel your love and your healing and restoring hand on me. I believe nothing stops you. If your plans for me are not worked out one way, they will be in another.*

I also noted in particular the words of Psalm 90:12: *Teach me to number my days aright, that I may gain a heart of wisdom.* I so much wanted to do what God wanted and nothing else—and I knew I needed more of God's wisdom.

Two days later, I headed for Joy's. It had been difficult to relax, yet I was still glad I had taken time off in an attempt to gain that heart of wisdom the psalm talked about. However, I was desperate to talk with Joy. I knew she would help me gain some much needed perspective, as well as encourage and pray for me. And I was also looking forward to sharing dinner with David and her and staying overnight in *The Quiet House* in their garden.

That night and the following morning, Joy listened to my impassioned account of how things had unfolded on team. Along the way, she offered several wise insights, which I jotted down for further thought. But it was the four questions she posed at the end that helped me look for a way forward rather than wallow in a mixture of self-pity and self-blame. First, she asked me to write down how I would like our team to function differently. Almost at once, certain things sprang to mind—it was like turning on a tap. I wanted more affirmation and encouragement in my role on team. I wanted various ministry structures to be finalised. I wanted more forward planning and prayer concerning our church's future. I wanted our team to be able to share our feelings more about our ministries and our church. Did we perhaps need the help of a consultant in all this? Or did we need to put aside more time for team-building?

I was on a roll now. One by one, I wrote down more things I wanted to see happen for me in ministry and for our team in general. I wanted more leadership wisdom and guidance in my ministry roles. I wanted us to be able to trust one another fully and have confidence we would do what we said we would do. And I also wanted a clearer mandate to pursue the ministries I believed God had called me to do.

My demands were many. As I wrote them all down, I could feel the anger and frustration being released. Yet I also felt somewhat ashamed. Did I have any right to demand such things?

Then Joy asked me to write down what I felt needed to happen for these things to become reality—a much harder challenge. I wrote, among other things, that I felt we needed to prepare better for our team meetings, to enable us all to give of our best and listen to one another. I believed we should engage the services of a consultant or team mediator to help us move forward in a positive way. I believed our senior pastor needed more administrative assistance and also needed to have some of his current roles lifted off him to enable him to focus on leadership and setting direction, both for the team and the whole church. And I also felt, on a personal level, that I needed to exercise forbearance and forgiveness, to risk trusting our church leadership again and to step out with more confidence in ministry.

I am sure Joy saw many other things that needed to happen,

although she confined herself to mentioning only a few. Chief of these was that I needed to continue to seek truth in our team relationships and not shrink back from being honest. This arose, I later realised, from her many years of experience within the community at Malabar, where members had learnt to be real with one another and face the truth about themselves. They had also tried to ensure their community was a safe place where people would feel accepted for who they were. And they had sought to put their own views aside and hear the Lord together, choosing to move forward in a way that was best for all. This involved listening to the Lord and also to one another. And, as Joy explained, it involved loving one another from the heart 'because he first loved us', then drawing others into the kingdom through this shared love. I had wanted this level of love, acceptance and trust in our ministry team from the beginning, but had not known how to bring this about. Nor had it been my place to do so.

Joy then challenged me with another question.

'Jo-Anne, I think what you have to ask yourself is, given the last four years of ministry and the current situation on the team, what things can you realistically expect will change?'

It was a good question and a much needed reality check for me. I had had such faith in our church and our leaders. I wanted it all to go well and for things to be different. But was I being unrealistic? Was I even deliberately not facing up to the truth?

'Well,' I mumbled, 'I'd have to think about that. I expect some good administrative help could be found for our senior pastor. And if the right consultant were found, that could help too. But whatever we do, it may well take a while for things to change.'

And then Joy put an even more confronting question to me.

'If that's the case, then do you feel you can still function in your role on team?'

I knew it was a fair question to ask, but it was not one I wanted to answer. I felt as if a dagger were thrust into my chest at the very thought and was silent for a long time.

'I don't know, Joy,' I responded after a while. 'Maybe in the end it won't be my choice, even though I've been called to our church for another five years. I'm not so sure I feel very wanted on our team right now.'

At that point, Joy sat up straight and looked straight at me.

'Well, whether they want you or not, they may not be able to *have* you!' she said in a very determined, almost haughty voice.

'Oh, Joy!' I laughed, despite myself. 'You're so good for me! I've never let myself think along those lines before this.'

Joy suggested she lead in a time of prayer and meditation before I left. As she did, I became aware of a deep anger inside me and a sense of being used. At that point, I saw a picture of Jesus holding a glowing, molten ball of lava in his hands, which I knew was my anger, and tossing it back and forth as if it were too hot to hold. At first, he was teasing me gently as he juggled that ball around, but at last he covered it with cloth so he could hold it better. I realised then that he had covered it with his own cloak and was drawing that ball into himself until it disappeared.

I had much to think about on my drive home down the mountains.

A month later when I again visited Joy, I realised there had been a big shift inside me since we had last met. I felt much less enmeshed in our team issues and in our church as a whole. While still caring about our future, I was now able to be a little more objective about things. As we talked, Joy helped me see the importance of understanding what was happening on our team and how this impinged on our willingness to forgive one another where necessary. We talked too about forgiveness itself—how it is as much about letting *ourselves* off the hook as well as the other person, and also how it involves letting go of the burden of having to make the other person pay and allowing God to sort it out instead.

'I do feel less burdened than when I was here last,' I told her. 'But let's wait and see—it's early days yet.'

I then went on to share something I had read in a book about the Enneagram that had given me more helpful insight into how I functioned.[14]

'This book mentioned how "achievers" like me tend to depend on others to unlock the "doors to life" for them, which can lead to a lot of frustration and anger and also self-criticism. I think I might have fallen into that trap a little with both my husband and our church leaders. I guess it's tied in with learning to believe in myself more as well. The book also talked about accepting responsibility just for our own lives and not anyone else's—and I know I've felt responsible for others at times when I shouldn't have. It can be very exhausting—and no doubt annoying as well for the other person.'

I was beginning to see how important it was to be true to myself, but I still had a long way to go. And any ground gained in that regard was tested when our church year began to get under way in earnest. Soon I found myself once again embroiled in emotionally draining discussions about my ministry role, but I still could not understand what was driving it all. And, for the first time, I realised I did not feel very safe in the midst of such discussions. I was on shaky ground—unsure what I could and could not say, supported yet not supported, wanted but not wanted. At one stage, doubts were expressed about where I 'fitted' in our church, which, rightly or wrongly, I took as a strong hint I was not needed anymore. Then one afternoon, I was told we could no longer continue working together.

I went home in a daze, convinced this was the end. But, by the next morning, the picture had changed again. Now, it seemed, I *was* still needed and was welcome to stay on after all.

Had I taken everything too personally, treating some things that were said as a huge, personal 'de-affirmation' when they had not been intended that way? Had I overreacted and made some big assumptions in it all? Did I repress people, as had been suggested? Was I too much of a 'mother' on the team—a perfectionist who demanded others measure up to my standards? Had my appointment to the team perhaps not been strategic from the very beginning, as was implied at one team meeting? I did not know anymore—I seemed unable to think with any great clarity at all. And, ironically, I realised that, just as I was about to move into areas of ministry I loved and believed I was gifted to do, I felt too emotionally drained to undertake them.

I knew something had to be done. The next morning, I phoned Joy and arranged to see her that afternoon. I cancelled my appointments for the day and decided to postpone a mentor training course I had planned to begin later that week. I needed to make some firm decisions and I was aware I needed help to do it.

That afternoon, I valued more than ever that safe place Joy managed to create for others. After welcoming me in her usual warm, caring way, she at once set about enabling me to state what I needed in order both to survive and move on in my role. I had always been reluctant to express my needs in any context. But I knew Joy was right—it was what I had to do. With her help, I managed to put together some brief statements, expressing exactly what I needed. These included postponing my mentor training course indefinitely and undertaking fewer responsibilities for the next three weeks, having a skilled intermediary meet with the team to work through issues, and embarking on some course of action as a team to enable us understand one another better. I also requested freedom to express my emotions within our team over the discord we were experiencing, since that was part of who I was. At first I felt ashamed to mention this, but, with Joy's help, I began to see that such emotional awareness, both within myself and others, was one factor that made me a better counsellor and mentor.

Strengthened by Joy's encouragement and supported by her prayer, I returned home and was able share these needs with our elders. They listened well and agreed to implement several measures designed to help us as a team, including meeting with both an experienced mediator and a Myers-Briggs consultant.

Around three weeks later, our team drove up the mountains for the initial meeting with our mediator. His first recommendation was that I take a month off from ministry. At any other time, I would have rejected such a suggestion. Surely this was a sign of weakness and an indication I could not do the role I had been called to do? But this time I was too tired to argue—and I knew Joy and my husband and family would agree with our mediator. On a much earlier occasion, Joy had shared a delightful piece of writing from *The Curly-Pyjama Letters* by Michael Leunig with me about taking time out to rest. In it, Mr Curly tells his friend Vasco Pyjama that unless he rests, he will become 'restless', and proceeds to encourage him to do nothing. I was indeed 'restless'—and I knew it was more than time for me to do nothing as well.[15]

But I also saw, as we talked with this kind but firm gentleman, that I had been my own worst enemy, trying to rescue younger team members when they neither wanted nor perhaps needed to be rescued. And I realised I had not set good boundaries for myself, something Joy had been trying to show me for some time.

That same week, our team also completed our Myers-Briggs type tests, driving together up the coast to meet with an experienced consultant. It was a good day as we realised how different our personalities were and what each of us needed in order to function well. Our results showed that two of us required plenty of prior notice before discussing important church issues, whereas the third member of our team was happy to develop his ideas as we talked. We were not wired the same—and we saw at last how important it was to take such things into consideration.

But the statement that rang most often in my ears as we drove home was some personal feedback our consultant gave me.

'Oh, you have to keep the boat afloat!' she said, looking at me in a kind but direct way.

That brief sentence summed up how I had been feeling for a long while. Whether that boat needed me to keep it afloat or not was beside the point—I had decided it did and had rowed madly, almost exhausting myself in the process.

My four weeks' leave was both relaxing and restorative, as I experienced again God's gracious and loving care. I stayed home for the first week, revelling in having no particular responsibilities. I read, listened to music, drove wherever I liked and cooked. I borrowed a video of an anniversary concert performance of my favourite musical, *Les Misérables*, at London's Royal Albert Hall and felt self-indulgent, as I watched it for hours. I sat lost in reflection as I read Henri Nouwen's *Out of Solitude* again and enjoyed the luxury of being with God in the midst of that solitude. And I marvelled at God's kindness in speaking so clearly to me from Psalm 3: *But you are a shield around me, O Lord; you bestow glory on me and lift up my head.* And as I flew to Brisbane at the end of that week to spend time with my sister, I knew God was watching over me and would again lift up my head.

My many conversations with my sister were vital in helping me work through things a little more. Just like Joy, she believed in me and encouraged me not to blame myself too much in it all. But some of my greatest insights came from the hours I spent reading my minister brother-in-law's books on the Myers-Briggs Type Indicator. I discovered that, with my INFJ personality, I tended to take things too personally when scorned and retreat inwards, blaming myself. I was often too idealistic, ignoring reality. I tended to stay committed to something for far too long, despite clear indications that it was time to move on. And I could also obsess far too much over hurtful comments or minor details. All of it was so true of me and gave me much food for thought.

During the last few days of my time off, at Joy's suggestion I attended my first conference on spiritual direction. Joy was there too, but with other friends of hers also present, I was content to make my own way, meeting new people and also enjoying being by myself. I appreciated the main sessions, taken by a brilliant author and theologian from England, Margaret Hebblethwaite, on the topic 'Ignatius for Today'. I enjoyed sharing with the many professional and committed women around my own age present and also with the men. I was touched by their complete acceptance of me as a woman in ministry and particularly moved when the men, including Anglican and Catholic priests, treated me with such grace and respect.

But there were two events at that conference that impacted me even more. The first occurred during a workshop on focusing, something I had wanted to learn more about ever since Joy had introduced me to it. In a brief group time of focusing, led by a Catholic priest, God spoke to me through a picture about what was happening on our team, urging me not to be pulled down by it all but to act with mature insight and grace. As our workshop concluded, I felt God's Spirit filling me in such a powerful way that, involuntarily, I sat up straight and squared my shoulders. It was a moment of profound relief, the impact of which I was to carry with me into the weeks and months ahead.

The second event took place during one of the chapel services held in a designated corner of our large meeting room. The chairs were arranged in a semi-circle, facing a beautifully decorated central table on which stood a large cross. I had arrived a little late and as I walked towards the candle-lit corner where the other participants were already gathered, I was almost overwhelmed with the sheer holiness of the moment. Some beautiful but unfamiliar music was playing, the mellow tones of the singers almost bringing me to tears. They were singing a version of Psalm 131:1-2:

> My heart is not proud, O Lord, my eyes are not haughty;
> I do not concern myself with great matters or things too
>   wonderful for me.
> But I have stilled and quieted my soul; like a weaned child
>   with its mother,
> like a weaned child is my soul within me.

I found it all so moving. I later discovered this music was written especially for contemplative worship by Margaret Rizza and hastened to buy two copies of the CD—one for myself and the other for David and Joy.[16] And when I returned to our church, I would often play it in my office as a gentle reminder of that day.

I was not to concern myself with matters beyond me. Instead, I was to rest in God's arms like a weaned child, allowing God to quieten my soul and give me peace as I went about my ministry.

Chapter Eight

Finishing Well

It was strange, but as I slipped back into my role at church, I began to feel both more uncertain and more fulfilled. Part of me was beginning to question whether I should continue on team, while another part was delighted to be preparing material I had long wanted to teach—input to our ministry leaders on the gift of prophecy and also my mentor training course which had been deferred. At first, things seemed to run smoothly on team, but it did not take long for old concerns to surface and the tension to mount.

Around a week after returning, I had a terrible dream which I shared with Joy when we talked the following day.

'I dreamt I was supposed to conduct a wedding and also provide all the food for the wedding breakfast, but nothing had been done,' I told her, crying as I felt the panic rising in me. 'It was so unlike me, as you know how well prepared I like to be. With only five minutes to go, I tried to organise the church folk to bring some food, but then had to rush to get ready myself. However, I couldn't find any suitable clothes to wear and my children were being more of a hindrance than a help as they started to put make-up on me. When I arrived for the service, I discovered I had to play the organ as well, but my music was all over the place. Then I realised I didn't have all the necessary documentation ready for the wedding ceremony—the certificate the couple were meant to keep was missing!'

I was sure Joy must be able to see horror etched on my face. And I realised I was feeling so embarrassed that I had let the bridal couple down and made the guests wait.

'It sounds like there's so much chaos in you and a real sense of being out of control,' Joy commented.

We prayed together and I felt more at peace. But I knew the dream was a warning from God and that something had to be done to avert chaos for me. Was it a simple case of taking steps to order my life better—or was some more drastic measure necessary? Was I meant to leave our church?

At the end of the following month, after discussions with our leadership, I cut back to halftime, which I hoped would ease some of the pressure I was feeling. My husband was sceptical, however, since the ministries I planned to continue involved almost as many hours as when I was fulltime. And deep in my heart, I knew I had not gone far enough. Looking back later, I believed this was a compromise on my part with God and all I could bring myself to do at that stage. I loved our church so much—probably too much.

Another month passed before I could face the thought of leaving altogether, but God made it so clear to me in the end that even I could not ignore what I had to do. One night at an elders' meeting, as the elders were praying for us as a pastoral team, I realised with alarm how removed I felt from what was happening. Then I heard God say: *'It's all too late, Jo. Close the door on this church. I have something else for you to do.'*

At our team meeting a few days later, I told my colleagues I was resigning. I then wrote a letter of resignation to our elders, something I found extremely difficult. And not long after, I again drove up to see Joy.

It never crossed my mind to wonder how Joy would receive the news of my resignation. I knew she would encourage me somehow— and I needed that. She had always responded with joy and delight to any breakthroughs or 'successes' in ministry I shared with her and empathised in my disappointments. And that empathy had worked overtime as far as I was concerned in recent months. However, her response to my resignation took me aback a little at first.

'Oh ... I'm *so* glad!' she exclaimed, with a sigh of relief and a roll of her eyes.

Joy's heartfelt reaction showed me clearly her depth of feeling on the matter. And as we talked further, I began to wonder how many times she must have bitten her tongue and wished I would decide to leave. But Joy had always been careful not to impose her ideas on me. She was the most gracious of spiritual companions, allowing me to make my own decisions in my own time. Yet in this instance, I was touched and encouraged by her relieved response. It showed me how much she had engaged with me on the long, emotional journey to this point of resigning and how much energy she had expended on my behalf as she listened to me and upheld me in prayer. But more than that, it was a huge affirmation to me that I had made the right decision. I had told our team and our elders at that point, but was yet to tell our church—and already I was having second thoughts. I needed all the reassurance I could get.

'I'm so glad you feel like that about it, Joy,' I told her. 'It sounds like you think I made the right decision.'

'Oh yes!' she said again, with fervency.

It was agreed that I would announce my resignation myself when I next preached in our morning service, but on the previous Sunday as I sat in church, I felt so isolated and so aware of the hurt, pained expressions on the faces of our elders. I had taken my resignation letter to each one of them individually, yet while they all affirmed me and said they understood, I could see I had disappointed them, especially one woman elder who was my closest friend. I was also well aware I had wounded our senior pastor by stating my reasons for leaving in such a straightforward way in my letter. It was a salutary lesson, when angry words about this were aired during a second team meeting with our mediator, to realise with blinding clarity how I had refused to trust my own judgement yet again. In my original resignation letter, I had decided to keep my reasons for leaving a little vague. However, in the end, after listening to the advice of two male colleagues, I had decided to be more explicit in what I wrote. Somewhere inside me, I still held onto the belief that the men must always be right.

I was so glad Joy had introduced me to the technique of focusing. One afternoon that week as I sat with God, allowing myself to feel the pain inside me, I saw a picture of a big screw boring right into the centre of my body, with pieces of flesh being ground out in the process. As I asked myself what the hardest aspect of that pain was, I realised the answer was that people had been and would be hurt by my actions. I had always hated hurting people and cringed at the thought of inflicting so much pain on those I loved who had trusted me and called me onto our ministry team. But, after a while, I sensed God saying gently: '*I can look after them.*' And I knew I had to leave it at that.

I needed that reassurance so much the following Sunday when I told the church I would be leaving at the end of the year. People were warm and loving and lots of hugs ensued, but it was very difficult. One older gentleman almost brought me undone with his heartfelt response:

'It's just like when Jesus told his disciples he was going away,' he said, wiping the tears from his cheeks.

Another gracious lady added further to my grief in trying to come to grips with her own.

'I'm so very sad you're leaving, Jo-Anne,' she told me. 'You *are* the church for me!'

Many precious comments came my way in the days ahead. One elder told me I was the heart of our church, the 'glue' keeping things together, the mortar around the bricks. But it was two words spoken with feeling by one of our younger members as only he could, that best summed up what I was hearing:

'*Monster* loss!' he said in a gruff voice, as he gave me a huge hug.

I was so relieved to be able to continue processing my grief with Joy. At one stage around then, I felt I should think more about the ways in which my own personality, words and actions had contributed to our team difficulties. Facing my own responsibility for these events would, I hoped, give me a better perspective on what had occurred and also stop me wallowing in a sea of self-pity. But I did not want to fall into the opposite trap either of blaming myself for everything. I was therefore very thankful for Joy's wise and loving input and her prayerful support through it all.

As we talked, I realised I had a deep and longstanding ownership of our church. I had been a member for almost eighteen years and owed so much of the richness of my Christian experience to many wonderful people with whom I had shared those years. Some were still there— and several of these were my close friends. Together we had seen our church go through many and varied crises, as well as exciting times of renewal. And together we had prayed long and hard for God to move amongst us and in those living nearby. Some things we had prayed had come about—but there was still much, much more we were hoping and praying God would do through us. Along with them, I had poured myself into our church—and, as a result, I was very protective of it. I did not want to see it damaged through unwise leadership or wrong decisions, so from my perspective, there was a lot at stake.

As a result, I realised I had felt threatened and tended to overreact and become too defensive at times, especially when my role in our church was questioned. And my sense of insecurity in ministry had not helped either. I had come to theological college late in life. Despite my informal ministry experience, I was still a new college graduate in my first paid ministry role. And I was also a woman. Besides that, I suspected, to my shame, that there was a considerable amount of wounded pride involved. I had been an A grade student throughout my life. I was used to doing things well. I was an achiever and a perfectionist. And I did not like being told I was not fulfilling my role well or that I did not fit.

But both Joy and I wondered if there was a spiritual component in it all too. In my distress and fear, I had at times lost sight of God and fought battles in my own strength. And I suspected I had allowed the enemy to distort my thinking, so that certain negative beliefs had begun to take on a life of their own in my mind. Over and over, I had kept hearing such strong, accusing messages that eroded my confidence even further. *'You don't fit here ... your ministry is not strategic ... you repress people ... you have nothing to offer in leadership.'* And I had allowed it all to worm its way into my spirit until I had felt disempowered and 'de-affirmed'.

It was heavy stuff. Yet God was gracious as I asked for forgiveness for my part in making things worse. I was determined to deal with these issues and to look to God for the strength to stay the course and finish well. There was much to do and I wanted to honour God's call and our congregation's trust in me. And Joy stayed with me as I sought to do that, supporting me and praying for me to the very end.

As it turned out, I experienced some of my most fruitful times of ministry in those last few months. I particularly enjoyed running my mentor training course—a project I had laboured long and hard over. Some of my ideas had come from the mentor training program I had been a part of at the end of my time at college, but I had also used a variety of books and resources. To these, I added material of my own that suited our own particular church context. But the course bore the hallmarks of my times with Joy as well. I had benefited so much from our journey together that I was determined to pass on this experience to others.

I decided that my best approach, given I would soon be leaving, was to invite twelve people who showed leadership potential or were already in a leadership role to take part. I ended up with ten women and two men, all of whom tracked faithfully with me throughout the course. Our training was three-pronged. Firstly, the course involved two seminars for the whole group, during which the 'basics' of mentoring were covered in an interactive way. Secondly, I organised three peer group experiences, with participants divided into two smaller groups of six each. In these groups, various listening skills were practised and 'mini-mentoring' sessions experienced in pairs. And thirdly, I committed myself to meeting three times with each participant during or straight after the course. Most had never had a mentor, so I wanted to give them at least a taste of a positive mentoring experience.

It was a huge undertaking at that stage of my ministry, but I enjoyed it all, especially the individual mentoring sessions. I felt privileged to be allowed into the hearts and lives of these men and women. As I talked with them, I often found myself smiling as I shared thoughts and phrases that reminded me of Joy. And I knew she would be delighted that something of our experiences together was now being passed on to others. At times I modelled Joy's use of silence, for example, in our small groups. And I also often found myself sharing poems or meditations I knew Joy loved. On one occasion, we listened to Margaret Rizza's version of Psalm 131 and sat in quietness afterwards, watching the flickering flame of the candle I had placed on a low table. And on several occasions I found myself using phrases about self-care Joy would often use—'Be kind to yourself!' ... 'Listen to your body!' I suggested to participants that they try to journal, even as I had often journalled about my times with Joy. And I tried to encourage them to step into all God was calling them to do, just as Joy had done for me.

In other aspects of my ministry, too, I noticed the outworking of the rich legacy Joy had left in my life. In my counselling and prayer sessions with people, I would often find myself praying as Joy would have prayed with me or using elements of focusing to help someone become more aware of what was happening in them. Sometimes I would recommend a particular book Joy had introduced me to or lend out my own copy. And on many, many occasions, visitors to my office would comment on different sayings or meditative writings Joy had given me that they noticed on my pin-board. In the end, I kept multiple copies handy so I could give them away.

Joy walked faithfully with me through those last months of ministry, but suggested I might benefit from seeing a counsellor to help me process some of the deep pain I was feeling. Joy had always been humble about her own ability to help me through difficult times and had made sure I felt free on other occasions to seek professional counselling. I had always resisted the idea—I was happy with her gentle, prayerful ministry to me as my spiritual companion. Now, however, I realised I had burdened her with so much of my grief over a lengthy period that perhaps I needed to do something about it for her sake as well as mine. I was giving out so much in ministry, particularly after our senior pastor went overseas for a few weeks, and it was taking its toll. While I tried to ensure everything I did was God-honouring in that time, I was aware of the strain of keeping so much turmoil inside me at bay. So this time I listened to Joy's suggestion and made an appointment with a counsellor and art therapist she knew.

I felt tentative as I approached the counsellor's home for that first session. I was by no means an artist and had never studied art at school. However, that day most of the session was taken up with a long, tearful explanation of my situation. From time to time, she would comment in a firm voice, I suspect to ensure I would hear. But one thing I did not miss was her unequivocal statement that she herself could not have functioned as part of our team. In her view, the situation was untenable. In the midst of my anguish about letting our church down and my strong sense of failure, these words were so reassuring.

'It hasn't been a safe place for you, by the sound of it,' she commented. 'You seem to have heard so many mixed messages—and that's very confusing and exhausting for anyone. Also, if you don't have a job description and little clear direction, everything becomes very frustrating and dissatisfying. All up, a very difficult situation, I'd say.'

My homework that week was to look for pictures and words in newspapers or magazines that I identified with on an emotional level and bring them to our next session. I went about it with my usual thoroughness and was soon shocked at the depth of grief and anger I felt as I snipped my way through various newspapers. I cut out pictures of a coalminer, battered and bruised after emerging from a tunnel collapse, and one of a Bali bomb survivor, grieving at a memorial service. I found a large advertisement of a woman standing in a forest beside a huge tree and surrounded by lush ferns and cut it out, unable to understand why it moved me so much. Some headlines also caught my eye—'*uneasy allies*', '*it's my life*', '*containing the rage*', while odd words here and there seemed to jump out at me—'*dismay*', '*sacrificed*', '*explosive*', '*mourning*'. I cried my way through sharing these with the counsellor when we next met and realised she was right when she sensed that the forest scene typified harmony and safety for me—something I had longed for in our team environment. She also encouraged me to express my grief and anger then and there—an exercise I found difficult but freeing.

At the end of our next session, the counsellor suggested I list the things I had needed to function well in our team, as Joy had. She felt that writing them down would help me 'disengage' and stop looking for them anymore—and she was right. In another session, we talked about my family of origin and how the huge self-doubt the counsellor saw in me might have developed. And she also pointed out, as Joy and I had seen already, how my self-doubt had probably spilled over into the team, causing my colleagues to feel pressured to succeed and do things right.

In our last session, we finally managed some art therapy, which, despite my lack of expertise in using brushes, paints and crayons, proved to be a very powerful experience. I began by vehemently scrawling purple and blue lines all over the large sheet of paper I was given, then covering them with a mess of purple, blue and orange paint. In tears by now and very angry, I drew a large wooden cross in the midst of it all and a red heart right at its centre, with white light streaming from it.

'What would you like to call your painting?' the counsellor asked when I had finished.

Without hesitation I responded, "'Costly Sacrifice'."

Yes, my pain and anguish were evident in what I had painted. I had wanted to serve the Lord and give my whole heart to our church, sharing the light and love of Jesus through all I did. But my picture held a secondary significance as well. I saw there that Jesus understood my pain because of his own suffering on the cross—and I knew he was holding me close to his heart.

CHAPTER NINE

RECOVERY

On my second last Sunday at church, I led our morning service for the final time and also chose to play the piano during communion—something I had loved to do when we first began attending the church eighteen years earlier. That evening, I spoke to the young people in our evening service. The following Sunday morning, I preached my final sermon. I found this particularly hard, as I had always felt so privileged to share God's Word with our church. When would I ever have this opportunity again? I spoke from Philippians 2 and 3 on the theme of holding onto the faith. I wanted to encourage everyone to keep short accounts with God, to look to others' interests, to be wholehearted and to remember the final goal. I felt God's empowering, although everything seemed a little surreal.

Next came the job I dreaded most—cleaning out my office at church. From the beginning of my fulltime ministry, my office had mirrored Joy's influence on my life. A dear friend had taken charge of redecorating it as a surprise for me, purchasing new curtains and other furnishings from funds donated by church members. She also knew my colour preferences and the things I liked about Joy's study. So she took care to add touches that would create a similar ambience—a purple candle, a pot plant, an arrangement of huge, crepe paper flowers in a vase, a rug in rich tones of purple and blue draped over the back of a comfortable chair. My young male colleagues derided it as far too 'feminine' a room, but as time went by, many women—and some men—mentioned how safe and comfortable they felt there. I was delighted. I had hoped it would reflect God's creativity and grace to others. And I hated the thought of leaving it all behind.

At last it was time for my official farewell. It was a beautiful evening. We laughed and cried together as we shared wonderful memories, many of which were encapsulated in an album of photos, cards and greetings later presented to me. But most touching of all were two brief video clips from girls I had mentored now living overseas. Our senior pastor had visited them while away and recorded their greetings specifically for this evening. I cried as I watched—I had tried hard to be for them what Joy had been for me. And I was overwhelmed when I was presented with a large bouquet of flowers and several beautiful gifts—an expensive, gold bracelet, a dainty ring with amethyst stones, a pretty Venetian glass pendant and an elegant, cut glass bowl and cheese platter. My friends who had chosen the gifts, again purchased from money given by our congregation, knew I loved jewellery but could never allow myself to buy anything too valuable. So that is what they bought. Except on rare occasions, I have worn my bracelet and ring every day since.

Our senior pastor also handed me a gift that night that I came to value very much—a handwritten letter in which he thanked me for my friendship, integrity, support of and belief in him. Among other things, he wrote:

> *Thank you for your insight and wisdom, your care for the details, your love of quality, completion and doing things well. You will probably doubt it, but I'll say it anyway—I've*

learnt a lot from working with you—things that will add
depth and wisdom in times ahead ... I know your care for me
has always been from the very highest intentions. You are
one of the most loyal people I know.

But perhaps the most encouraging aspect of the evening was that both Joy and David had driven down to be there for me. It gave me great pleasure to acknowledge their presence and thank Joy publicly for her loving support. But it was also reassuring to be able to seek out her face when I stood to respond to all the encouraging comments and to thank our church for their gifts. I knew Joy had wanted to visit our church on several occasions when I had preached, but it had never quite worked out, which was in part my fault. I felt I had wanted her to be removed from our church—someone safe I could go to with no connection to anyone in my circles. For me, Joy represented another way of living out our faith in God that was precious and unique. And I wanted to savour that difference.

My remarks were brief that night, but I shared how I was going to have six months' break before embarking on any other ministry. Or perhaps I would write, I told everyone—something I had always wanted to do. I also shared how I felt I had left many things undone and incomplete, but had ministered as best I knew how. And, even in the hardest of times, I had felt so privileged and honoured to be called by them and entrusted by God to minister at our church. I had not believed it could happen—but God had brought it about and I was sure God could also lead me in the next phase of my life, too.

I did indeed feel confident of God's leading, because only a few days earlier I felt God had said to me: *Yes, your ministry here was a privilege, Jo-Anne. And I have another wonderful privilege for you down the track—but you might have to wait a while.* Could that be writing, I wondered?

Everything around me felt surreal. I was so glad I could go away to stay with my sister and her husband who had now moved to Townsville. Sitting on their wide, front veranda and gazing across the beautiful, blue expanse of water to Magnetic Island, I reflected on various Scripture passages and tried to hear God. What was I to do next? Was it time to fulfil that deep desire to write that I had talked about for years? I was too tired to think about it at that point, however. Now was the time, I knew God was saying, to take care of myself and relax. Yet there was one thing I was determined to do—and that was to continue meeting with Joy. I knew I would need her support to tackle whatever it was God had next for me.

I managed to catch up with her again at Christmas before my husband and I flew to New Zealand for a holiday. I was still numb from saying goodbye, but was aware of some remaining bitterness and self-blame over not handling issues better on team. Yet, in my burnt out state, I did not seem to have the emotional energy to do anything about it. I knew I would get through this time and needed to be kind to myself in the midst of all my swirling emotions. And I knew I had to accept God's grace and forgiveness for myself as well as extend it to others. I knew that in my head—but my heart needed time to take it on board.

Joy encouraged me to let God care for me and restore me, but also to look forward to the future in a positive way, rather than becoming stuck in a negative place. Not long after, she sent me the poem *Wide Open* by Dawna [Davna] Markova, with its clear challenge not to '*die an unlived life*', but instead to 'inhabit' our days and risk our significance.[17] I wanted that too for my own life. I wanted to honour God with all that was in me, but I was too tired and sad to do more than believe better days would come and trust God to hold me close in the meantime.

I tried to do justice to the amazing beauty I saw all around me in New Zealand as my husband and I explored parts of the North Island, but in my tiredness and grief, I believe I saw only a portion of that beauty. I enjoyed it all at surface level but could not seem to let it penetrate my heart and bring as much restoration as we had hoped. A large part of me seemed somehow frozen—immobile and out of reach.

One day, as I reflected on this, I recalled the two pictures I had drawn at Joy's so long ago, depicting where I was then in ministry and where I wanted to be. I remembered the chasm I had drawn in which I was stuck and also the large hand of God rescuing me. In the second picture, I was on solid ground again, tackling one ministry role after another. And nearby I had also drawn a hammock, suspended between two trees. We had assumed this referred to my recent time off, yet now I sensed it might well be speaking of my current situation. In my drawing, I remembered I was curled up in the hammock, fast asleep. Yet, as it again became clearer in my mind, I saw Jesus sitting with his back against one of the trees, gently rocking the hammock. At times he would stroke my forehead or hold my hand, just as one would do with a small child. And I sensed that as he sat there, he was guarding me, keeping watch on my behalf.

Had this been what the picture meant? Were the ministries I had hoped God would walk through with me still to come? Or did they represent the books I had been thinking about writing for so long?

There was only one thing I knew at that point about my future ministry. I did not want to apply for another position on a church pastoral team. The very thought made me feel even more exhausted.

On returning home, I soon found time to visit Joy again. Joy loved the picture of Jesus rocking the hammock and reminded me of it many times in the weeks ahead whenever I felt guilty about doing nothing. One thing she did suggest I undertake, however, was a course she herself had done several years earlier at the Aquinas Academy. This Academy was set up by the Marist Fathers and, being close to Sydney's central business district, aimed to be a school of spirituality in the heart of the city, accessible to anyone seeking to explore questions of faith. The Academy offered a variety of courses, some more biblically based and theological and some more reflective and contemplative.[18] And, despite my tired state, I was interested from the outset. The course Joy suggested I do, 'Developing Your Own Spirituality', involved attending a two hour lecture and open forum session each Wednesday morning, with the option of taking part in a small group discussion prior to each lecture. I saw this as a good opportunity to hear input from a different perspective. And I could even combine it with enjoying lunch in the city with one of our daughters or exploring nearby bookshops.

I joined a small group of around ten participants, led by a friendly Josephite nun, while our lectures were given by an erudite, outspoken Marist priest. The material was highly philosophical and contained some theological terms I had never encountered before, but I appreciated the lecturer's approach and the gracious way he led our open forum times. I loved having my mind stretched in this way and relating to the various thoughtful, professional men and women present.

As part of our group work, we were provided with 'readers'— collections of essays and articles linked to the lecture topics—one of which we discussed each week. On one occasion we read a parable by Rollo May, *'The Man who Was Put in a Cage'*.[19] In this story, the caged man is at first angry at the king for putting him there, but gradually accepts his fate and, in the end, becomes insane. As we discussed this story, God reminded me of my picture of the tiger in a cage and of Joy's comment that I was keeping myself in that cage. The emotional impact this brought with it was so strong I found it hard to speak—I saw again with shocking clarity how terrible it would be to accept such entrapment. Our group leader, noticing my silence, asked me if I had anything to add and, although somewhat overwhelmed, I managed to share what had impacted me. Afterwards, she and I talked for some time and her empathy and understanding were like soothing oil to my spirit. I felt so blessed to be listened to with respect and to have my cage picture taken seriously.

But this gracious nun was to bless me in an even more profound way. At the conclusion of our final group meeting, she suggested someone lead us in prayer and smiled in my direction. I thought she was asking the nun next to me to pray, but nothing happened—at which point I realised she was smiling and nodding at me.

'Yes, I mean you, Jo-Anne. Would you please pray for us all?'

I did as she asked—I loved praying for people. But afterwards I felt overwhelmed. Here was I, one of the few Protestants present, being asked to pray for the others, including two nuns! I felt so honoured. And, in this concrete way, I believe our leader was acknowledging the call she could see on my life—to pastor and pray for others. It was a beautiful but bittersweet moment and reminded me how much I was missing this role. Later, several of the women shared how they had appreciated my prayer for them—the Holy Spirit, the Comforter, was indeed present in that group.

But this course impacted me in another important way as well. Through the articles in our readers, I was given a taste of the works of so many interesting authors, some new to me and others I had long wanted to read. I discovered Flannery O'Connor, Annie Dillard, Esther de Waal, Basil Hume and the Jewish writers Elie Wiesel and Abraham Heschel. And I reacquainted myself with Thomas Kelly, Victor Hugo, A J Cronin and Graham Greene, to name a few. All this not only broadened my spiritual horizons but I believe helped prepare me for my own writing journey to come.

I was so thankful Joy had encouraged me to do this course. Many times I was to share with her the things I was learning and experiencing there. And that year, Joy also encouraged me to attend my second spiritual direction conference. Again, meeting and talking with men and women from a variety of Christian traditions was stimulating, but it was the understanding I experienced in our 'quad' group that I valued the most. On one occasion when reflecting on the input we had heard, we were asked to talk about a time when we functioned out of our 'false self' rather than our 'true self'. As I shared some of my experiences on team and my eventual resignation, it became obvious I was still grieving. To have a wise Anglican minister present comment that by resigning, I had made a good decision out of my 'true self' was so reassuring. But it was the gentle response of a young woman there that brought the most healing. I had shared how I reacted out of my own insecurity and self-doubt to hurtful comments said at the time and that I could still hear in my mind the words 'I can't see where you fit'.

'You know, Jo-Anne, I think that might be very true,' she told me.

'What do you mean?' I asked, bewildered.

'I'm sensing God didn't see where you could fit there anymore either—so it may well be a very positive statement. You're bigger than that! God has a better place for you—somewhere that's just the right fit.'

On another occasion, we were asked to divide into pairs and share our call or vocation. I found myself paired with an elderly nun and told her how lost I felt after leaving our church.

'Try to savour that "lostness" and see what God is saying to you through it,' she told me. 'You may never experience it again.'

She also encouraged me to reflect on Jesus' own 'lostness' and how he never really fitted anywhere while on earth. These were new thoughts to me—so comforting and profound.

But God brought comfort to me in another way at that conference. At one stage, we were encouraged to spend time alone, being mindful of what God might be saying through the things around us. I chose to go to the chapel and found there a wonderful, artistic, three-tiered display. On the top level was a gold cross, while on the second, a beautiful flower arrangement had been placed, its blossoms trailing down to the third level, where a large candle was burning. Behind all this, some purple and red satin cloth had been draped in a way that made it appear to flow down from the cross straight towards me as I sat, mesmerised. How beautiful this 'sacred moment' was, enabling me to hear what the Spirit was saying and receive more of God's grace!

I stayed there for a long time. I knew God was holding me close and calling me to be all I was created to be. Earlier, we had taken part in a special communion service, during which we were invited to anoint the person next to us and say to him or her, 'Be not afraid to be who you are!' As those words were spoken to me, I had realised afresh that if God had created me and given me certain gifts, then it was up to me to be fully 'Jo-Anne' in return. Now I felt God was giving me permission to go on my own, unique journey, wherever it might lead, in the power of the Spirit.

Chapter Ten

New Perspectives

What that journey would entail was soon to unfold in a surprising way. Around two months later, I found myself heading for Turkey to visit a friend I had mentored for some years. She had emailed, asking me to pray for someone to share a brief holiday with her. As soon as I read her email, I sensed God wanted me to offer to go. I was free. I had the time. And I wanted my friend to have this much needed break. I had visited her once before, but she had now moved to a small town where things were quite difficult. Perhaps I could stay on afterwards and help her for a while, I decided. My offer was accepted—and soon I was busy preparing for my next trip to Turkey.

We travelled by bus from my friend's home town to Antalya, then headed west along the Mediterranean coast. One morning towards the end of our trip, we each decided to spend some time alone with God. I picked up my Bible and began reading Isaiah 42, taking up where I had left off. I noted verse 9 and copied it into the small notebook I had with me:

'See, the former things have taken place, and new things I declare; before they spring into being I announce them to you.'

I then wrote the following: *Lord, I know the former things are gone, but please open my ears to hear you announcing the 'new things'!* I kept reading, but halted when I came to verses 18-20:

'Hear, you deaf; look, you blind, and see! Who is blind but my servant, and deaf like the messenger I send? Who is blind like the one committed to me, blind like the servant of the Lord? You have seen many things, but have paid no attention, your ears are open, but you hear nothing.'

A few moments earlier, I had asked God to open my ears. Surely these verses were speaking straight to me?

Later, I told my friend what had happened. At first, she seemed stunned by the verses I read out.

'What do you think God's saying to you?' she asked in a cautious voice.

'I know God's rebuking me—but it's such a gentle, loving rebuke,' I told her. 'You know how I've been talking for a long time about writing? Well, it's as if God's saying in a somewhat exasperated tone: *Come on, Jo! How many times do I have to show you? Go home and start writing the book!'*

I had loved writing all through my school and university days. In my early thirties, I joined a writers' group and had one short story published in a Christian magazine, but both the writers' group and the magazine folded soon after. After meeting an older Czech woman at the church we were at then and hearing her story, however, I told my husband I would write a book about her experiences one day—never thinking I ever would. Yet I continued talking about writing this book for years, until my family became tired of hearing about it. At one stage, my older daughter gave me some books on writing as a birthday present, together with a pen, a notebook and a homemade bookmark, decorated with a steaming cup of tea and the inscription: *Write your own!*

At my recent farewell, I had mentioned my desire to write. I had already told friends I had ideas for five novels, the first being based on the experiences of the Czech migrant from our old church. She had long since passed away, so I could not write her biography, but I hoped I could create a novel from what I knew of her story. Then in the months leading up to my trip, I had talked on and off with Joy about starting to write. And now here was God telling me to see what was right under my nose—that this was at last the moment to begin writing. I would not be wasting my time—*this* was what God was now calling me to do.

Not long after I returned, I caught up with Joy again. I wanted to tell her what God had said, but I was also looking forward to giving her something I had bought for her in Turkey—a deep red and black pashmina wrap, featuring a typical Turkish design. I had suspected she would like it and was not disappointed.

'Oh, it's so beautiful!' she kept saying. "That's far too big a gift to give me!'

I wished I could have given her much more, but I knew nothing could repay the time and effort she had put into supporting me over the years.

I began to describe some of the places my friend and I had seen on our travels. We had started our journey in the Apostle Paul's home town of Tarsus and had travelled through the areas of Cilicia, Pamphylia and Lycia and towns such as Myra and Patara, all mentioned in Acts. We had also enjoyed several amazing days at Antalya, the 'Attalia' of Acts 14:25, before travelling on as far as Datcha and then heading inland. Joy was intrigued to hear about it all.

'What a wonderful experience, Jo-Anne. Imagine seeing all those places we read about in the New Testament!' she said with some envy.

'I'll never forget Datcha,' I told her. 'It's near Cnidus, the place in Acts 27 where Paul had difficulty getting ashore. We stayed in Eskidatcha, or "old Datcha", a quaint, little village nearby—and I believe God spoke to me there through some words in Isaiah 42.'

I went on to explain what had happened. Joy had always affirmed my desire to write and was now even more convinced I could do it. However, I still needed much encouragement in the months ahead to commit myself to the task and believe I could write something others would want to read. I took my first tentative steps, reading books about writing and planning out my novel, but found it hard to grasp the challenge with both hands. I was moving forward—but the past still had a grip on me.

Around that time, Joy suggested I read the book *Scarred by Struggle, Transformed by Hope*, by Joan Chittister, a Catholic nun who had always wanted to be a writer.[20] At one stage in her late twenties, Joan had been encouraged by her Superior to apply to study for a Master of Fine Arts degree in creative writing. However, later the same Superior told her to withdraw her application—she did not consider her ready for such study. Instead, Joan was sent as a cook to a children's summer camp, a job considered 'better for her humility'. As I read, I was challenged by the way Joan rose above this huge disappointment and how she learnt to regard it in a more positive light as '*the gift of beginning again— conversion*'. She also wrote about the need to let things go, however unresolved or unjust or disappointing they might be, so that our present was not consumed by our past and that joy would be '*given the chance to surprise us again*'. She wrote too about the concept of re-inventing oneself, of becoming '*the rest of what we are able to be*'. I had been given a unique opportunity to re-invent myself, I realised as I read—or perhaps to allow God to re-invent me—and I needed to grasp it with both hands.

Joy also encouraged me to read again a favourite of mine, *A Testament of Devotion* by Thomas Kelly.[21] What I read there reinforced the things I had learnt from Joan Chittister, especially with regard to dealing with disappointment. While I was becoming more excited about the new challenge ahead, I had still been grieving the loss of that ministry role. I therefore took heed when Kelly wrote about meeting disappointment successfully, '*enriched rather than narrowed by it*'. I needed to remember how much my ministry role had taught me— and also realise how much even my grief at leaving this behind had enriched my life experience.

I set myself the task then to reflect on what I called my 'sabbatical journey' and to write down the things I had learnt in this time of recovery and of waiting. I also decided to share my conclusions with Joy, as well as with a trusted ministry colleague concerned about how I was travelling after leaving our church. I had re-discovered so many things about God, I realised, as I sat down to write my list—*God's love is so deep and abiding; God is so patient with me and protective of me; God understands me completely; God is a God of hope and new beginnings; God delights to speak to me; God believes in me; God is so full of grace and mercy; God brings healing and comfort in so many ways, some quite unexpected; God's kingdom is a lot bigger than our church; God has a unique journey ahead for me that will utilise all of who I am and harness all my gifts and past experiences.*

My list of things I had learnt about myself was even longer. *First and foremost,* I wrote, *I belong to God and can rest in God's amazing love for me.* It was just as well I could, I realised again, as I then went on to list several negative discoveries about myself: *I have harboured a lot of self-doubt that has affected not only my ministry but that of my colleagues; I have had a deep belief that the opinions of others, particularly men, must be right and my own must be inferior or wrong; I tend to feel responsible for things for which I am not responsible at all; I try to 'rescue' and protect people too much.* Other statements I wrote described how I was feeling and were more positive in tone: *I miss very much the love and friendship of people at our church; I am happy working alone, but also need a small group of people around me who believe in me and can be trusted to speak into my life; there are still places of real hurt and disappointment in me, but also a growing hope for the future; I have gifts, abilities, insights and wisdom gained from experience that are needed to build God's kingdom; I don't want to waste time being less than 'Jo-Anne' for God or doing things that are not very significant for God's kingdom.*

I was encouraged to find I could write not only negative but also positive things about myself, as was Joy, who had often tried to foster more self-belief and self-acceptance in me. As a child, Joy had often felt she needed to 'measure up' and reach a certain standard. Then, as a young woman, she had struggled to be herself and feel accepted. She was helped in this, I came to discover, through Camp Farthest Out, in which participants were taught to accept themselves and one another and to honour the gifts God had given each one. She and others undertook many creative activities at these weekends, such as poetry writing and drawing, not apologising when their artistic efforts might leave much to be desired, but rather looking for what God was saying through these 'creative acts of God's grace'. Joy's involvement with the community at Malabar also reinforced this acceptance of self and the life God had given each one. On one occasion, she shared with me something she had heard in a course about 'doing' community that both challenged and inspired me.

'When we get to heaven,' she told me, 'we won't be asked "Why weren't you Moses for me?" or "Why weren't you the Virgin Mary for me?" Instead, God will ask us, "Why weren't you Joy—or Jo-Anne—for me?"'

I was convinced then that I should use my God-given writing gift to the full—I needed to be 'Jo-Anne' for God. Not long after, while again visiting my sister in Townsville, I came across a book of meditations by Craufurd Murray, entitled *Cherishing Christ*.[22] In looking at the parable of the talents, he noted the wonderful confidence shown by God in investing creative gifts in us. Again, I realised I should not ignore my writing gift but instead honour the trust God had placed in me. The difficulty, however, was putting what I believed into practice.

Towards the end of November, my husband and I attended a pastors' day at a nearby conference. During the first session, the speaker began to give prophetic words to people. To our surprise, he turned to us and announced:

> *I see for my brother and sister here that there's been such a restlessness, a frustrated restlessness, but what I hear the Lord saying is that your dry season is over, your wilderness is over. This is a year of advancement, this is a year of strides, this is a year of progress, and it's like I see the enemy throwing so many*

*fiery missiles—if it's not one thing it's another coming at you different ways—but you are going up into a new level. This coming year there is going to be more accomplished, there's going to be more progress, there's going to be more strides, there's going to be more satisfaction than you have seen in years. And the restlessness—that's a divine dissatisfaction—is from God. But I tell you, if you had a lot of time on your hands before, I hope you enjoyed it, because those days are over, praise God. Those days are over, glory to God, and God is going to ... it's like a catapulting you into more. You're going to find more of your destiny, you're going to hook up to the vision, and I see so **many** things coming into place. Praise God, praise God. Hallelujah, we thank you for it Lord!*

My husband felt the word was much more for me than him, since it seemed to fit so well with what was happening in my life. Along with all my grief and questioning, there had indeed been a growing restlessness. They way ahead had been made clear while I was in Turkey, but I was still unsure I could do what God was calling me to do. Months later, I became convinced this word had in fact been accurate, as I experienced the great satisfaction that came from writing and felt in my heart I had 'hooked up' to God's vision for this stage of my life. But at that point, I was still restless and unfulfilled. I suspect Joy must have often wished I would take hold of such a God-given opportunity to do what I had always wanted to do and get on with it. Instead, she listened patiently each time we met and walked with me step by step as I set out on this new writing journey.

At first, I found it hard to get used to working alone, writing in a kind of vacuum and answerable to no one except God.

'I love being by myself,' I explained to Joy. 'I can be self-disciplined—and in some ways it's quite freeing to be my own boss. On the other hand, I don't really know what I'm doing, so it would be good to be reassured I'm on the right track at times. I guess I won't know that until someone edits my book.'

'I can imagine it must feel like no one's there to cheer you on,' Joy commented. 'It's a rather hidden work, isn't it—a bit like mine. I meet with a few people such as you—and I pray. Some time ago, I felt God showed me this "hidden journey, hidden work" was what I was to do at this stage of my life. Most of it takes place alone or just with one other person like you—it's not out there for all to see.'

'I do miss interacting with others and being "up front",' I responded. 'I think working alone can lead to all sorts of self-questioning. So many times I wonder if I'm going about things the right way or even if writing's a "legitimate" use of my time.'

'Yet you know this is what God's called and gifted you to do,' Joy reminded me. 'I suppose it's a matter of being with God in it all, isn't it?'

'I think I know what you mean. I'm becoming more conscious of God always being there beside me as I write. Sometimes I even pray out loud when I don't know how to write something. And I know I'll have to trust God to help me find a publisher when I finish my book.'

Joy would sometimes say things that would stay in my mind long after and continue to encourage me. On one occasion around this time, she talked about 'finding the gold and letting it happen'. That stayed with me as I let myself become more and more immersed in my writing, delving deep into my heart and mind to find the 'gold' and express it. I was slowly learning to let the words 'happen' and flow as they seemed to want to. On another occasion, Joy described my call to write as a 'tall space' God had given me—something a little out of the ordinary. And as I contemplated these words, I appreciated yet again Joy's priceless gift of believing in me and believing God could call me to write.

I became even more indebted to Joy when she introduced me to the writings of the American Christian author Madeleine L'Engle. I had come across her young adult novel *A Wrinkle in Time* when teaching high school English classes over twenty years earlier and had loved her beautiful, imaginative writing. Now I discovered she had written over forty books, including adult fiction, biographical works about her family and her marriage, poetry, commentaries on Scripture and books of prayers and reflections. I borrowed several from Joy and especially loved the *Crosswicks Journal* volumes. But my favourite by far was L'Engle's reflections on faith and art entitled *Walking on Water*, containing insights into how she approached her own writing.[23]

At first, I identified with this book through a misunderstanding of its title. Since I was still in the early stages of my first novel, I saw the words 'walking on water' as a very apt description of my writing journey at that point. I felt uncertain I could do it and so insecure, just as Peter might have felt in the story in Matthew 14 where he attempts to walk towards Jesus on the water. What Madeleine L'Engle was trying to convey, however, was the wonder of that glorious moment for Peter when he forgot his doubts and strode across that water towards Jesus in faith. She maintained that we too can experience these moments of miracle—of being transported to another realm, if we get rid of our adult scepticism and listen, look and believe.

Yet my initial misunderstanding turned out to be a happy accident, because I soon realised I identified with so many of L'Engle's thoughts about writing, particularly its close link with prayer. I was delighted to read that, for her, working on a book was much the same as praying. L'Engle wrote how the author's main task was '*to listen to the work, and to go where it tells him to go*'. In the same way, she also believed prayer was more about listening to what God was saying rather than talking ourselves and asking for things.[24]

When I read these thoughts, I heaved a sigh of relief. I was also at home in prayer and, over time, had learnt to listen to what God had to say to me concerning my personal life and ministry. So I had tended to approach my writing in the same manner, often asking God if I was heading in the right direction. Then I would try to listen to where the story needed to go and do my best to take it there. But I had been asking myself for some time if this was a legitimate way to write. Should I be doing something different? Should I stop writing until I learnt more about plot and structure and characterisation and other facets of novel writing I was yet to master? Once I discovered that

Madeleine L'Engle approached her writing in a similar way, however, I relaxed—my approach was legitimate after all. Knowledge and skills were also important, but this listening was indeed a vital part of good novel writing.

Other observations in this book were also helpful for someone as new to writing as I was. Already I had discovered that, after having planned out my novel, the story often ended up taking a different direction. Characters I had not thought of including would pop up and even threaten to push their way to the fore in my storyline. L'Engle understood this process, I discovered, and even considered it a necessary part of the whole imaginative journey. She also talked about having no choice but to immerse oneself in the work one had been given—a feeling with which I was becoming more and more familiar. At times I had felt carried along by the very story I was trying to create, as if it had a life of its own. I could not have abandoned it, even if I had wanted to—it was now part of me. L'Engle validated such feelings and thus increased my confidence as a writer.

As the year drew to a close, people began to ask what I planned to do with my life. The question that irked me most was, 'We know you're writing ... but what do you *do*?' But a story included in *Walking on Water* helped me see the funny side of such questions and realise how little understood an author's life can be. L'Engle tells how, when she was at last receiving good royalties for her work, someone commented to her how most people would have to work hard to earn such amounts![25] While some of my friends understood the many hours involved in writing, others could not seem to see it as 'real work'—and I had to learn to accept that.

I had changed so much in my 'sabbatical year'. By God's grace, I had faced my pain and grief and learnt much more about myself. It had been a watershed year—one in which my life had taken a whole new direction. I had matured spiritually and emotionally. And Joy had been a vital part of all this growth and change, believing in me, encouraging me, providing me with good resources, suggesting conferences and courses I might like to attend. I was not alone in being convinced that writing was what God had for me to do next.

But I knew that as I continued down this path in the coming year, I would need Joy's ongoing warm encouragement. It was not going to be easy, by any means.

CHAPTER ELEVEN

PROGRESS

I began the new year in a frustrated state. I had made inroads into writing my novel, but had also realised what a mammoth task still lay ahead. And I planned to visit Turkey again at Easter, taking a younger woman with me. Trips such as this took time to organise, but on top of that, I had been trying to learn Turkish for some months—or enough at least to get us by until we linked up with our mutual friend living in Turkey. I was finding it hard to balance these diverse activities—not to mention minding grandchildren and normal household tasks. I knew God had called me to do the things I was doing—but I was not tackling them in a peaceful way.

One afternoon, in the midst of all my busyness, I saw in my mind a picture of Jesus carrying me though a 'no man's land' area in the middle of a war zone, weaving his way around shell holes and trying to dodge bullets raining down on us. Jesus took some of the bullets in his own body but was determined to keep running. I realised then I was injured—I was so floppy in his arms.

This was how I felt, I told Joy, as I recounted my picture to her during my first visit that year. I knew Jesus was protecting me and would never let me go—but I felt bombarded and well aware I was in enemy territory.

Joy reminded me that Jesus must have felt so much frustration during his ministry here on earth. He had to walk by faith, keeping his eyes on his Father God. I knew I needed to follow his example—it was the only way to do what God was calling me to do.

I was also aware my frustration was exacerbated by those old, niggling feelings of self-doubt. Did I have an inflated opinion of myself to think I could be an author? I was beginning to enjoy writing, but was still unsure whether I was going about my novel in the 'right' way as I identified with my characters and allow them to shape the story.

'Do you think this is all "okay"?' I asked Joy, after describing what was happening and how alive I felt when I had uninterrupted time to write.

'Yes, of *course* it's okay! In fact, I think it's *wonderful!*' she responded, without a moment's hesitation.

I tried not to burst into tears. I sounded like a child, waiting for that reassuring 'Wow! Well *done!*' from a parent, and felt a little ashamed of myself. But I knew Joy meant what she said.

Around that time, my husband and I were invited to a party at the home of an elder from our old church. On the whole, I received a warm welcome from the many old friends present, but some did not seem to know what to say to me. I felt clumsy and awkward—as if there were no 'niche' for me among them anymore. And I encountered not only the now familiar question of 'We know you're writing, but what do you *do?*' but also a slightly different one—'We know you're not in ministry now, but what do you *do?*'

'I didn't know what to say,' I told Joy, still fuming. 'My initial feeling was guilt—but then I began to feel quite angry. What do they mean by "ministry"? I'm assuming something official like being on a church pastoral team—but surely what I'm doing is still ministry?'

I went on to share with Joy some things I had read in Philip

Yancey's book *Soul Survivor.* In a chapter about the American Christian author and ordained minister, Frederick Buechner, Yancey describes Buechner's study in a farmhouse in Vermont, noting how it's as if Buechner is '*leaning on an invisible pulpit*' addressing '*an invisible audience*' as he writes. On the next page, Buechner himself describes his writing as a disorganised and unstructured ministry, but still, he hoped, '*a legitimate one*'.[26]

'That's how I feel about my writing,' I added. 'I don't have any books published yet, but I often have that sense of leaning on a pulpit addressing an audience out there somewhere when I write. I don't aim to preach at people through my novels, but I still hope they are drawn close to God through them.'

Joy understood how I felt from her own 'hidden work' of spiritual direction and prayer. And she also reminded me again how essential it is to learn to follow the unique path we are called to take, despite what others say.

'People won't always understand what you're doing, but you can't do anything about that. It's important to trust your own judgement and do what God's gifted you to do.'

I remembered then a card I had bought not long before. It said: '*She who trims herself to suit everybody will soon whittle herself away.*' I knew I had to stop seeking everyone's approval—I was not to 'trim myself' according to what others thought and lose the real me I was beginning to discover. I told Joy how I had rather defiantly placed the card near my computer where I would see it often. I had been a 'people pleaser' for far too long, trying to fit in with others and shape myself and my ministry around them. Now I was free to take up my own unique challenge.

As soon as I returned from Turkey, I again immersed myself in writing. I also decided to attend some seminars at the New South Wales Writers' Centre, as I had the previous year. I knew I needed to understand more about preparing a manuscript submission and also about the various publishing options available. While these seminars were helpful, they also delivered a solid reality check. The market was hugely competitive, I was told—there were so many manuscripts out there and only a few were ever accepted. And it was particularly difficult for first time authors to penetrate the market. Sometimes these seminars left me discouraged, wondering why on earth I was wasting my time writing a novel. I might never find a publisher. And we did not have the financial resources to undertake self-publishing or subsidy publishing.

Yet, despite such discouragement, I knew I had to keep on writing. I was well into my novel now and determined to press on. Besides, I was discovering how much I loved losing myself in my writing for long stretches at a time. Yet some days were hard going. Sometimes I would write several pages, only to delete them the next day. And often I would spend hours researching to make sure every detail in my novel was correct. How long, for example, would it have taken to travel by train from Tábor to Prague during the war years? Was it even possible? Was a particular town in Czechoslovakia taken over by the Germans at the time my characters were there or not? What were migrants to Australia told about their new country in the holding camps in Germany? Sometimes I would find myself procrastinating, unwilling to commit to sorting out some problem or other in my manuscript. But how could I both love and hate writing? How could I be a 'real' author?

It was a relief to discover after a while that other authors often felt the same. One day, Joy lent me *The Joy of the Snow*, the autobiography of her beloved novelist, Elizabeth Goudge.[27] I was soon reading how this well-known author described the process of getting a book out of one's head and onto paper as grinding slog. She also maintained she had heard of writers who had to be locked in their studies to induce them to start writing!

The difficulties I was encountering were far outweighed, however, by the deep fulfilment I began to feel as I immersed myself more and more in my novel. The story was a sad one to write, since it centred around the grief and loss suffered by Heléna and her family and friends in Czechoslovakia during and after World War Two. But, in a strange way, I found the experience cathartic as far as my own journey of leaving our church was concerned. My loss was nothing like the horrendous losses recounted in my novel. Yet I was able to identify with my characters in their grief and was conscious God was using this to help me deal with my own grief. And it was also cathartic on another level. I had loved my ministry role at our church. Yet I discovered a whole new level of satisfaction and fulfilment in my writing, which took me by surprise. I had wanted to write for a long time, but never suspected I would love it so much.

'It's like I'm somehow fully "alive"—like I've grown larger on the inside,' I tried to explain to Joy. 'This might sound strange, but when I look at the trees and shrubs in our backyard from where I sit writing, they seem greener and somehow more defined, as if I'm seeing them in 3D. It's like this whole creative experience has brought me closer to nature—or perhaps closer to our Creator God. It's amazing!'

Joy was the only person I knew who I sensed would understand this, being so creative herself. She had grown up surrounded by music, learning the piano and enjoying singing. She had loved dancing at a young age and would make up her own steps, which in later years developed into worshipping via creative movement and liturgical dance. She understood the power of drama and art in worship and of expressing our whole selves—mind, body and spirit. She enjoyed writing poetry, some of which I had read and loved. Joy understood the great fulfilment true creativity could bring, especially when used to honour God, and was pleased I was discovering this for myself.

'You seem to be finding yourself in a much deeper way,' she commented one day. 'What you're experiencing reminds me of that quote from Irenaeus—"*The glory of God is a man* (or woman!) *fully alive*"'.[28]

I had not heard these words before and loved them. On my next visit, Joy lent me a book by Jesuit priest Anthony de Mello entitled *Awareness.* In it, I stumbled on the phrase, the *'awakened person',* which I felt described well this heightened sense of alertness I was experiencing through writing. De Mello defined this awakened person as someone who 'dances to the tune of music that springs up from within'.[29] I related well to that description—there were so many ideas bubbling up inside me. And I remembered the words of the American philosopher Henry Thoreau: 'If a man loses pace with his companions, perhaps it is because he hears a different drummer. Let him step to the music which he hears, however measured, or far away.'[30] Yes, I did still feel somewhat alienated when others did not understand what I was doing or see it as 'ministry', but, as my writing journey unfolded, this began to matter less and less.

My enjoyment of writing continued to deepen as I completed chapter after chapter of my novel. Some days were still hard as I wrestled with how to keep the story moving at a good pace, but I sensed I was beginning to get there. I had thought I would have difficulty reaching a hundred thousand words, which was my original target. I was now well past that but there was still so much more to write. I pressed on—I could not have stopped even if I had wanted to. I felt so fulfilled, yet in the midst of this fulfilment, I still had to do almost daily battle with that accusing, critical voice within, bearing all the hallmarks of the enemy.

The place where I did the bulk of my writing was at our kitchen table, facing a china cabinet with glass doors. Sometimes when I caught sight of my reflection in those doors, I would hear that mocking voice inside my head. *Look how old you are! Why would you think you would ever get published? Who's ever going to want to read something you write? Why are you sitting here writing anyway? You left a perfectly good ministry position—people needed you there. Why don't you go and do something useful?*

Over time, I learnt to ignore this voice and choose to hear God's voice instead, speaking wonderful, encouraging words into my spirit—words that built up rather than tore down. *I love you, Jo! I'm so delighted to see you doing exactly what I've called you to do. Keep going! Don't give up!*

When Joy and I were discussing this issue one day, she reminded me of the occasion in John 12 where Mary takes a large container of pure nard, an expensive perfumed oil, pours it on Jesus' feet and wipes his feet with her hair. After I returned home, I read the passage again and the words that followed. While Judas Iscariot objected to wasting the precious perfume and pointed out how the proceeds from its sale could have been given to the poor, Jesus did not see it that way at all. In fact, he rebuked Judas, declaring that while the poor would always be among them, *he* would not. Just as Joy had tried to show me, I sensed Jesus saying that the effort I was putting into my writing was not wasted in his eyes. All the time I spent researching and crafting my novel was in fact my own 'perfumed oil', poured out for him. How blessed I was to be able to 'waste' these efforts on Jesus!

Yet even stronger than the fear that I might be wasting my time was my fear of failure—the very thing the enemy had wanted to stir up with that sneering question I had heard so often, '*Who's ever going to want to read something **you** write?*' One day, however, I read a section in *Walking on Water* where Madeleine L'Engle was pointing out how, whenever we set out to create something, we run the risk of failure. If we were not prepared to fail, we would never accomplish anything. I knew I had no guarantee my book would ever be published, but unless I tried to complete it and submit it for publication, I would never know whether it could be done. Besides, if I believed with all my heart I had been called to write, I needed to keep trusting God in it all. I was not wasting time—and I need not fear failure either.

By August that year, my novel was almost complete. As I checked and re-checked it, tweaking sentences here and there and deleting whole paragraphs, I smiled when I saw how much Joy had influenced some things I had written. At one point, I had Heléna's future husband quoting Julian of Norwich's words '*All shall be well, and all manner of thing shall be well*' to Heléna, soon after meeting her—words I had first heard from Joy. At another, I had written how Alexandr, Heléna's teacher at the Prague Conservatorium, would always encourage her to believe in herself, just as Joy had often done for me. And I saw, too, how similar some of Heléna own comments about issues she faced were to various comments Joy had often made to me. Other characters in my later novels were to resemble Joy even more, but by then, this was a deliberate choice on my part. With this first novel, however, Joy's influence seemed to have crept in almost without my noticing.

The date and even the time when I finished the first draft of my first novel are noted in large letters in my journal for that year. At 11.20am on 3rd September 2004, I wrote:

> *FINISHED NOVEL* HELÉNA! *Unbelievable feeling! Thank you so much, Lord! Now for all the hard work, 'mopping up', organising, editing and following up leads re publishing. I know you will be with me throughout the journey, however. As you have been, so you will be. Amen!*

Early that afternoon, I phoned Joy.

'Joy, I've finished the book!' I burst out, almost before she had time to register who was calling.

'Oh Jo-Anne, that's *wonderful!*' she responded. 'How do you feel?'

It was such a delight to share my news with her and pour out all the emotion of the moment to her. Later, when I told others, I would receive a lukewarm response at times—something along the lines of 'Oh, that's nice!' In reality, I knew they could not be expected to understand the euphoria I was feeling. But Joy did. She had journeyed with me every step of the way and had believed all along I could do it, encouraging me to believe it as well. And to have someone just as excited as I was about it all was a wonderful confidence booster.

Two days later, I received a card from her with beautiful, blue irises on the front. Inside was written:

> *'The Book! Well done, dear Jo-Anne. Congratulations—**and** my prayers and love for the next phase. Joy'*

I treasured that card in the days ahead. I knew the journey of receiving feedback from my manuscript readers and trying to find a publisher would be arduous. But I also knew Joy would stick with me over the long haul, praying my first novel through to publication.

Others were also praying on my behalf for that elusive publisher. But one day in a women pastors' retreat group, I heard one of the younger women present pray for my book in a way that touched my heart. This girl treated my novel as a real child I had conceived and laboured long and hard over. With great fervency, she prayed that my 'baby' *Heléna* would be brought safely into the world and even dedicated her to God.

'I think I can understand,' she told me later, when I tried to thank her through my tears. 'You know, I'm sure I saw a new Christian publisher advertised in a magazine I was reading the other day. Did you see it too?'

I shook my head.

'I was reading it at my mother's place—I'll look it up next time I go there and send you the details,' she promised.

I thanked her, but in my heart doubted she would remember. After all, she had three young children and many responsibilities in her church. Only a matter of days later, however, she emailed me the details as promised. Little did I know then that this would in fact be the very publisher who would accept my novel for publication. But there was still a long journey to go before that day arrived.

CHAPTER TWELVE

WAITING

At first, I was too eager for my own good to see my novel published. Without waiting for all the feedback from my manuscript readers, I submitted my masterpiece to a well-known secular publisher, who rightly rejected it. Fingers burnt, I then waited until my four manuscript readers were ready to give me their comments. It was no small task I had set them—my original version of *Heléna* contained a hundred and seventy thousand words! I had chosen readers from different age groups so I could see whether my novel had broad enough appeal and as each returned my manuscript, I tried to take every suggestion on board.

Their comments were all helpful and wise, but I soon discovered I was still a 'people pleaser'. I worried my manuscript readers might be offended if I did not put all their suggested changes in place. And I tortured myself even further, wondering if the positive comments they made were sincere or merely meant to encourage. I rewrote and rewrote. I studied how to write a good manuscript proposal. I purchased a copy of *The Australian Writers' Marketplace* and went through every publisher listed, noting any who would accept an unsolicited submission from a first-time author without a literary agent and coming up with around five. At last, I again sent off the first three chapters, plus the further information required, to the first secular publisher on my list. At the same time, I parcelled up my whole manuscript and sent it to the new Christian publisher my friend had told me about.

I heard back with almost indecent haste, I felt, from the secular publisher. They were sorry, the letter read, but my novel did not appear to 'fit' their publishing list. I decided to plough on, trying the second secular publisher on my list. Again I waited, only to hear they had decided not to release any more novels that year. However, this time I also received an encouraging note, telling me they saw potential in my writing and congratulating me on completing such a long novel. With my heart sinking, I tried a third secular publisher and received another swift response—my novel was not what they were looking for. I then tried a second Christian publisher. I decided that if I did not hear back from either Christian publisher within a certain time, I would try overseas.

Joy kept on encouraging me each time we met, reminding me to continue trusting God in it all. Again, I reflected on how much I owed her. Then one day, while reading some information from the Sydney Symphony Orchestra, I saw a special Beethoven concert advertised. It was The Sydney Symphony Season Opening Gala event, featuring the Philharmonia Choirs alongside the Symphony Orchestra, plus a guest pianist, soprano soloist and three other singers. The program was to begin at seven in the evening and last for an amazing four hours. It included Beethoven's Fifth and Sixth Symphonies, a piano concerto, two sections of the Mass in C, Beethoven's Choral Fantasy for piano, chorus and orchestra, and a recitative and scena for soprano and orchestra. This huge program replicated a concert Beethoven himself had conducted on 22 December 1808 in Vienna, despite his increasing deafness, to premiere his latest works.

'Wouldn't that be wonderful?' I commented to my husband. 'It would be a unique experience, but it's a bit expensive.'

Since he was not a great classical music fan, I expected him to give the advertisement only a cursory glance. But whether it was my excitement as I told him about it or the fact that I had just returned from another special visit with Joy, he came to me a while later with what at first seemed an outrageous idea.

'Why don't you take Joy to this concert?' he suggested. 'We could give her the ticket as a thank you for all the time she's spent with you. She could stay with us overnight.'

I knew Joy loved classical music—particularly Beethoven. She and David had attended chamber orchestra and symphony concerts together in the past, but had been unable to do so for some time. Besides, Beethoven was *my* favourite composer too. What a delight to share such a momentous event with Joy!

I decided to phone her to see if she would like to go.

'Oh, that would be *wonderful*!' she exclaimed, with an ecstatic sigh. 'But—are you sure?'

We were sure. When the day arrived, Joy was able to get a lift to the Opera House and we met up in the foyer. We joined other excited concertgoers seated in various spots on the steps of the Opera House to eat our packed dinner of sandwiches and fruit, then made our way to our seats in the dress circle. We looked at each other, finding it hard to believe we were inside the Concert Hall, waiting for such a glorious feast of music to begin.

It was an amazing evening, beginning with the Pastoral Symphony. To our surprise, one or two people near us left during the first interval. How could they do such a thing, we wondered, when there were so many more delights to come? The brief recitative, the Gloria from the Mass in C and Beethoven's Piano Concerto No 4 followed, after which quite a few more people around us left. It was already late, but we stayed on. We were not going to miss one note of our wonderful, musical treat. Next came the Symphony No 5, followed by Sanctus from the Mass in C and, last of all, the Choral Fantasy. It felt somewhat bizarre to be sitting in the Opera House as the clock ticked on towards midnight, listening to a massed choir and orchestra whose members must have been so exhausted. But when the conductor put his baton down at last and slumped against his stand, totally spent, we clapped and roared our approval. We felt so privileged to have witnessed such a performance and knew we would never see or hear anything like that again in our lifetime.

Around midnight, we headed down into the Opera House car park and drove home through almost deserted streets. I was concerned Joy might be feeling exhausted, but she did not seem to be. Both of us were still somewhat lost in all the music, still wanting to savour the magic of the moment. As I drove, I felt privileged to be able to give Joy such a wonderful evening and to take her home now with me. She deserved much more, but I hoped she would remember our shared experience with delight for years to come. Once home, we crept into the house like two giggling schoolgirls, trying to be quiet and not be found out. Our adventure was over—but I knew each little memory of it would remain with me forever.

The following morning, our son arrived early with our granddaughter, Amy, whom we minded each Friday. After breakfast, we bundled her into the car and drove Joy back home. Later, Joy sent me a card with the following note:

> What a special night it was last Thursday! Thank you so very much for inviting me, for having me stay the night **and** bringing me home again. It was wonderful to experience such a breadth of Beethoven's work and to witness such a performance.
>
> Jo, it is a joy to me to know you. Thank you for these years of being able to walk with you a little.
>
> Would you thank Tina (our daughter) for her comfortable bed? I hope Amy enjoyed the rest of her day with you both, and you with her, and that you weren't too tired at the end of it!
> Grace and peace,
> Much love
> Joy

I marvelled again that God had given me such a faithful, spiritual friend. Who would have imagined Joy would still be accompanying me on my spiritual journey and that we would have continued to enjoy each other's company so much?

As the year progressed, I began to despair I would ever find a publisher. There was only silence from the two Christian publishers I had approached and I was almost out of options as far as secular publishers were concerned. Eventually, I entered a writing competition which offered entrants a phone assessment of the first three chapters of their manuscript with one of the competition's judges. I was determined to listen to everything this editor said.

'Jo-Anne,' he commented at one stage, 'I don't have any particular faith, but I see you've spent time in some sort of church ministry. So ... where is the religious aspect in your book?'

'Well ...' I hesitated, 'I decided not to mention religion or Christian things much in the first few chapters. I didn't want to alienate my readers too early in the piece.'

'Oh no!' he told me with feeling. 'Religion's a good topic to write about. But I think you need to begin your story in a different way. Don't start with Heléna already here in Australia and flash back to what happened to her in Europe. Get straight into the story.'

Crestfallen, I looked at my first three chapters yet again. Yes, they were clumsy and forced, I decided—and with a resigned sigh, I deleted them and began all over again, this time including a reference to God in my first sentence. If I had to rewrite these chapters, I would write exactly as I wanted to.

Inspired with a new confidence, I submitted my manuscript to a Christian publisher in the US. Yet again, however, it was rejected. At that stage, I decided all I could do was wait to see if one of the Australian Christian publishers would still respond and, in the meantime, read up on self-publishing.

I was not good at waiting, which must have been obvious to Joy when I complained about it yet again during one of my visits.

'Could you view this waiting as an *active* time—perhaps even an honourable activity?' she challenged me one day.

It was such a simple but radical change in perspective for me to see waiting as part of the whole process and accept it, refusing to let it frustrate me. Joy also suggested I look up Habakkuk 2:3-4—some verses I later discovered had been key for them in their community at Malabar:

> For the revelation awaits an appointed time; it speaks of the end and will not prove false. Though it linger, wait for it; it will certainly come and will not delay. See he is puffed up; his desires are not upright—but the righteous will live by his faith.

I saw again I needed to keep on trusting God and wait patiently, without wavering. This was further emphasised in another passage Joy pointed out to me—Isaiah 30:15-18:

> In repentance and rest is your salvation, in quietness and trust is your strength, but you would have none of it.
> You said, 'No, we will flee on horses.' Therefore, you will flee! You said, 'We will ride off on swift horses.' Therefore your pursuers will be swift!
> A thousand will flee at the threat of one; at the threat of five you will all flee away
> till you are left like a flagstaff on a mountaintop, like a banner on a hill.
> Yet the Lord longs to be gracious to you; he rises to show you compassion.
> For the Lord is a God of justice. Blessed are all who wait for him!

While this showed me I was not to run around trying to make things happen in my own strength, I did not envisage I was to sit around idle. I would keep my eyes open for a publisher, but listen well to God in the process, moving when I felt God said to and not before.

As I waited, I decided to fine tune my skills through short story writing. I knew my writing style was very wordy—after all, I had grown up on a diet of the 'Anne' books by L M Montgomery, *Little Women* by Louisa M Alcott and the others in that series, the 'Pollyanna' books by Eleanor Porter and many more of a similar nature. I loved the verbose style and long sentences of Georgette Heyer's novels and the wonderful prose of Dorothy Sayers. But my own style needed refining and 'de-cluttering'. I then decided to enter several of the many writing competitions on offer around Australia, realising the discipline of having to write only one or two thousand words by a particular entry date would help. I did not win anything and was highly commended only once, but I found the experience invaluable.

At last I risked letting Joy read one or two of what I considered my best short stories. The one I suspect she related to the most was entitled '*Mister Santa Claus*', a sad and whimsical story which was my favourite, too. In it, I wrote about Colin, a marginalised man from South Brisbane who loved to dress up as Santa Claus each Christmas. Thus attired, he would give out gifts bought throughout the year to children at local shopping centres. Colin was particularly proud when he turned fifty-two, the longest anyone in his family had ever lived. A young couple from a nearby church tried to look after him, but not long after they moved interstate, Colin passed away. When they returned to sort out his belongings, they found his original birth certificate, which showed he was only forty-nine. I had been inspired to write about Colin by my nephew, who worked with marginalised people in South Brisbane and had told me the story. I suspect it struck a chord with Joy, bringing back memories of her own involvement with such people in Surry Hills. And I felt pleased she found it so moving.

That year, I travelled to Turkey again to be with my friend and together we explored the mountainous north-eastern area along the Black Sea coast and further inland. I loved it all, but always in the back of my mind was the issue of what was happening with my novel and where I needed to turn next with it. The trip unsettled me a little too, in that I wondered whether I should be spending so much time writing, with so many other things needing to be done for God's kingdom.

What if the hours I had spent writing came to nothing? What if my novel never saw the light of day?

At that point, Joy suggested I work my way through a book she had recently journeyed through herself again, *The Artist's Way* by Julia Cameron.[31] I had owned this book for some years but had never explored it properly. I was determined to do what Joy suggested, disciplining myself to write the three hand-written 'morning pages' required each day and completing the set tasks at the end of each chapter. And as I began, I was amazed at how well Julia Cameron seemed to understand my struggle to allow myself to be an author. She knew about my self-questioning and my doubts about my writing gift. Early on, I read about our *'abandoned self'*—that creative part of us that was not allowed space to grow. The author also talked about *'shadow artists'*—those people who find it difficult to allow themselves to explore their creativity and who do not take themselves or their gifts seriously. I related to it all, partly because my writing had already begun to open up a place inside me that seemed to have been asleep. Now I sensed I needed to wake up this creative side of me even more and give myself permission to explore avenues of creativity I had ignored for so long. I could also see I needed to give myself permission to be a beginner again, to make mistakes and even to fail. Even if my first novel was never published, at least I had tried and discovered how fulfilling it was to write.

It was wonderful how Joy understood the creative and spiritual journey I experienced through this course—this *'pilgrimage home to the self'*, as Julia Cameron termed it. It was quite foreign to me to think of my responsibility to care not only for others but also for myself and to spend time writing about my own needs and desires. But at least by that stage of my writing journey I had realised I needed to use my God-given gifts to the full. The author commented in one place that our gift back to God was to use the creativity we had been given rather than give it back unopened—and I believed this. But getting this from my head to my heart was still a struggle at times. In many ways, I was still that 'blocked creative' described earlier in the book, the one who tries to please others rather than care for her own soul, the one who wants to be 'good' and fit in, the one who feels guilty when spending time on creative pursuits.

One of my first tasks in this course was to 'blurt out' on paper all the negative core beliefs I held about myself. I decided I would be honest and was shocked at the result. How could I as a child of God still hold onto such self-doubt and negativity? I therefore grasped with both hands the opportunity given later in the chapter to turn these negative beliefs into positive statements of affirmation. Some of the key ones I wrote were:

- *I am being self**less** rather than self**ish**, being prepared to sit for hours writing, with no immediate reward, in the hope that my stories will touch and heal people.*
- *I have achieved a great deal in my writing over the past two years.*
- *Whatever failures, real or imagined, I have had or mistakes I have made, they are forgiven. There is no basis for shame in my life.*

I was now launched on a journey of self-discovery that would spur me on to continue writing and help me understand the reasons for the deep fulfilment I experienced as I did.

Around that time, I discovered almost by accident that one of the Christian publishers to whom I had sent my manuscript was no longer in business. I was now down to one potential publisher, so decided to search for a literary agent to represent me in the United States. My early attempts at this came to nothing, however, since I soon discovered it was almost as hard to find an agent as it was to find a publisher. Soon I abandoned the whole idea.

In the light of this, I valued Joy's continued encouragement even more as the weeks progressed, with still no response from the remaining publisher, and also as I continued to work through the various concepts in *The Artist's Way*.

'Your writing is so honouring to God, Jo-Anne,' she told me. 'It is the best way you can serve others—you are doing it for the sake of the Gospel. And if you don't let yourself write, how is that serving the gift? Your desire to write is God calling you—and you need to be obedient to that voice.'

Joy also encouraged me to be kind and compassionate to myself whenever I heard those negative messages in my head that still often tried to discourage me. She suggested I 'befriend' the scared child within me who was often so unsure about doing new things and thinking in different ways. She also quoted some lines of a poem to me from a favourite book of hers:

> The rose has no 'Why'
> The rose blooms because it blooms ...

I had no option, I realised. Just as the rose was made to bloom, I was made to write. It was something God had created me to do—and I needed to be faithful in that. One of the tasks set down in the fourth week of *The Artist's Way* course was to write my own 'artist's prayer'. With great emotion, I wrote the following:

> Lord, you're the Life-Giver, the Creator of everything—and
> I am made in your image. Thank you for your life flowing
> in and through me. It is all gift and I do not deserve it, but
> I receive it from your hands with my own open hands. I
> receive it and I will honour it and use it well as you show me
> how. Lord, may I follow you with all I have, listening for your
> voice, as you bring to birth the people and places and events
> you wish me to create. Be my Deliverer and the Deliverer
> of your creation through me. Fill me with your Spirit, Lord,
> continually—your creative, life-giving Spirit. Amen.

As I was making this journey of self-discovery, I was also puzzling where I fitted as far as church was concerned. I had spent three years attending a large church not far from our home while my husband conducted two interim ministries some distance away. It was now still impractical to go with him each Sunday to the church where he was then ministering, but I wondered if I should move to a smaller church in a more needy area. My thoughts about organised, structured church had changed somewhat, I discovered, as I undertook my lone writing journey. I found myself seeking something different—perhaps something more personal and life-oriented than program-oriented.

When I discussed this with Joy, she made several pertinent observations. She could see I had begun to allow all my insecurities to surface and be dealt with in much greater depth in recent months. Referring to the time on our ministry team when I was so confused about the 'shape' of my role, she pointed out how I now had my own 'shape' and was also far less concerned with titles or roles. Was this a time then when I needed to remain free of such things? Was this the moment for me realise it was enough just to be me, Jo-Anne—to be all of who I was for God?

'I sense God saying there are so few willing to do what you're doing—writing, learning Turkish and serving God in unique and fresh ways,' Joy commented. 'Could you perhaps learn to savour this freedom and just "be" with God? Yes, it's a time of instability, but this is all part of the process. Can you accept where you are with thanksgiving and be at peace about it?'

Joy also posed some further questions to think about. What was I looking for in a church or Christian community? What did I need and what was underneath that need? Were there other Christian writers I could contact and perhaps meet with? These were good questions that set me on a path of seeking out the fellowship I needed and thinking and praying about what church was to mean for me in the next phase of my journey.

Chapter Thirteen

Publication

Throughout this period, I continued to try different forms of writing. As well as my short stories, I completed a chapter book for nine to ten year olds, but was never very happy with it and put it aside in favour of writing another novel for adults. This was much more my genre, I realised at once, with a sigh of relief.

For some time, I had wanted to write a novel inspired by the friend I had met years earlier at the prayer ministry school who is blind. While I planned to write a novel rather than her biography, I wanted my 'heroine' to have the same courageous, fighting spirit and the same strong faith in God as my friend did. Joy was delighted with the idea— this girl was very special to both of us. And thus my second novel *Laura* began to take shape.

Around that time, I also attended a writers' festival, mainly to help me decide the next step to take with my first novel. I had given up on hearing back from the Christian publisher my friend in the retreat group had told me about. After all, it had been over ten months since I had sent my novel to them. At the festival, I heard an editor speak who seemed competent and helpful. I later discovered she was a Christian and decided to ask if she would assess my *Heléna* manuscript. She agreed and quoted me a price of several hundred dollars, which I decided would be worth it at that point.

I printed out my lengthy manuscript and sent it off, along with my cheque. But that same afternoon, after waiting all those months, I received an email from Ark House Press, the Christian publisher I had decided was never going to contact me.

The email said they were interested in publishing my novel.

My first reaction was disbelief. I summoned my husband to check if I had understood the email correctly.

'Are you *sure* it says, "We are interested in publishing your novel"?' I asked him, my whole body shaking. 'Perhaps they mean "*not* interested". Do you think they've left the "not" out by accident?'

No, it was real, I discovered a few days later, on enquiring further. I would hear from the publisher again early in the new year, I was told, and would receive my contract then.

Joy was delighted, but also cautious. She knew how much my novel meant to me and did not want me caught in some shady deal that would end up costing me money. I valued her concern on my behalf—she had walked this writing journey with me and did not want my dream shattered in any way. I was able to set her mind at rest, however, as I knew Ark House Press was a legitimate, traditional, Christian publisher, producing books that seemed to be contemporary and professional.

I was glad to give Joy some good news. She often looked tired when I visited her now, as David's health had become a real concern during the previous few months. He had fallen more than once in the night during this time and Joy had found it impossible to lift him, since he was a lot taller. As it turned out, they were able to receive some ongoing home nursing help, but things were still not easy. Unbeknownst to me, she and her daughters had had to search for a suitable nursing home for David in preparation for the time when he could no longer be cared for at home. This thought upset Joy, but meanwhile, she struggled on, doing all she could to make David comfortable.

Then on 15th February that year, a young friend from our church passed away, aged only twenty. We were all devastated—it was a tragic event. We had prayed so much for her recovery and her family had left no stone unturned in trying to find a cure for her illness. Emily was a beautiful, intelligent and creative young woman who, despite her illness, had agreed to be my youngest manuscript reader. I suggested she read just a few lines of my novel at a time so it would not tire her out, but she finished it in two days. When she gave me my manuscript back, I found a little smiley face drawn on the front, with the words 'well done—ten out of ten' written beside it. At her memorial service, it occurred to me that the least I could do would be to mention her on the dedication page of my novel. I had decided months earlier to dedicate my novel to Joy, but now I resolved to add a note about Emily as well.

Joy did not know Emily but grieved with her parents and family in their loss. Each time I visited her, in the midst of her own grief about David's failing health, she still remembered to ask after them. And Joy also often enquired about our older daughter, now divorced and living in the inner city. One day months earlier when my daughter and I took a trip up the mountains, we had called in unannounced at Joy's on our way home. I was so moved at the warm way in which Joy welcomed our daughter that day, despite never having met her. In our brief time together, I could see how Joy must have touched the hearts of many a stranger in the past as she ministered Christ's love to them.

By this stage, I had managed to write around half of my new novel *Laura*. This project had proved quite time-consuming, as I researched many medical and educational issues related to visual impairment. This involved contacting not only eye specialists and artificial eye-makers but also organisations such as the Braille Association, the Royal Institute for Deaf and Blind and the School of Distance Education, as well as children's hospitals and special schools in Brisbane where the novel was set. This was a delicate subject to write about and I wanted to ensure any facts I included were accurate.

Yet all this came to a grinding halt one day when I received a disturbing email from my publisher. 'We think your novel Heléna is too long,' they wrote. 'Would you consider dividing it into two?'

I was horrified and annoyed, to say the least. Firstly, this novel had been accepted for publication in its entirety, so it did not seem fair now to 'move the goalposts'. Secondly, I doubted I would be able to re-write the second half in a way that would enable it to work as both a sequel and a stand alone novel. Thirdly, I felt it would annoy my readers by leaving so much up in the air at the end of the first novel. And fourthly, I was already well into writing *Laura* and did not want to change tack in order to re-write *Heléna*.

In the end, I resigned myself to the inevitable, listened to my publisher and agreed to try, due in no small measure to some reminders Joy gave me during my next visit to her.

'What do you think God is saying to you in all this business about dividing your book into two?' she asked me gently. 'And don't forget Proverbs 3:5-6.'

In my frustration at having to pour more work into my first novel, I realised I had taken my eyes off God and focused on the problem instead and my reaction to it. As Joy had suggested, I took a step back to see what God was saying through it all. I turned to my Bible and read Proverbs 3:5-6:

> *Trust in the Lord with all your heart and lean not on your*
> *own understanding; in all your ways acknowledge him, and*
> *he will make your paths straight.*

It was not all about what I thought I could or could not do. I was not to 'lean on' my own abilities, but instead trust God to work it out.

'You don't have to strive to prove yourself—just rest and receive from God,' Joy encouraged me. 'And remember—creation itself seems to have been a slow process!'

I laughed and felt myself relax inside. Joy was so good at seeing the bigger picture—and also at observing positive changes in me, encouraging me so much in the process.

'It seems to me you're growing up so much more into what's there inside you that could not be expressed before,' she observed later in our time together. 'And that's wonderful!'

Joy was still managing to walk my journey with me, despite her increasing concern for David, who had now been diagnosed with dementia, along with Parkinson's symptoms. In recent times, his health had deteriorated. Sometimes when I arrived, I would greet him as he sat rugged up in the lounge room in his favourite, old armchair.

'David, Jo-Anne's here,' Joy would tell him. 'We'll be talking for a while.'

'Oh, hello!' he would say to me with his usual, gentlemanly charm.

I doubted, however, whether he remembered me.

'Will he be okay by himself, Joy?' I would ask as we headed for her study. 'I don't mind if we sit in the lounge with him.'

'No, no, he'll be fine,' she would assure me, her voice firm but sad.

I wished I could do something more for them both in the midst of such a difficult period. One day, I mentioned how I had been given my own DVD copy of *Les Misérables in Concert*, the wonderful performance of excerpts from my favourite musical at London's Royal Albert Hall. This concert celebrated the tenth anniversary of the musical's original performance and featured a 'dream cast', including many original performers, and the Royal Philharmonic Orchestra. At the end of the concert, the flags of seventeen nations where the musical had been performed were carried onto the stage and the men who had played the role of Jean Valjean there each sang a line of the song '*Do you hear the people sing?*'

'That sounds so wonderful,' Joy told me. '*Les Misérables* is David's favourite musical too, but we haven't seen that DVD.'

That week, I bought them a copy and posted it off with great pleasure. Whether David was still able to appreciate what he saw and heard, I was unsure, but I felt it was worth a try. Something might strike a chord in his memory—and I was sure Joy would enjoy it too.

Once I had agreed to divide *Heléna* into two, I put everything aside to tidy up the first three-fifths of the original novel and prepare it for publication. At least there was some sort of clear break in the story at that point, with Heléna boarding the migrant ship to Australia. I was still unhappy at leaving my readers up in the air, but realised I had no other choice if I wanted my novel to be published. I was then left with the task of fashioning the remaining two-fifths of the original manuscript into a second novel of similar length. How would I ever do it? My response for the moment was to put such a daunting task aside and concentrate instead on trying to finish *Laura.*

I had struck some problems in writing this new novel and decided to discuss them with Joy, since she also knew the girl who had inspired it. My main issue was how to craft a novel while still remaining true to my friend's real story—my thoughts about this were becoming very mixed up. Did I have the right to add as much material as I was now adding from my own imagination? Or would this disappoint our friend? What if she did not like how I had depicted the main character? What if she felt my novel dishonoured her own story?

Joy counselled me not to worry about the real story and felt it was better to distance myself from the actual events in our friend's life. And as it happened, this turned out to be wise advice.

Not long after, I emailed our friend, now living overseas, the first five chapters of *Laura.* She had asked for them and explained how she could read them using her VoiceOver screen reader. I was happy to oblige—after all, I wanted her to check whether I had made any mistakes in describing how a visually impaired child would behave and manage her life. Her response came back quickly—and it was straight and to the point. She felt I had made some classic mistakes and common assumptions about visual impairment and let me know this in no uncertain terms. In one way, I was grateful to her—I did not want to offend anyone by what I had written. I knew my friend had radical views about how visually impaired people should be treated and often stated them with force. I admired her for this and also realised she would not have achieved what she had in her life without being so strong and determined. But her comments discouraged me so much, I almost gave up the project.

Joy kept encouraging me to write what I wanted to write—*I* was the author, not our mutual friend. And she reminded me again that I was writing a novel, not a biography. As a result, I emailed my friend, letting her know how I felt and we worked through it. And in the end, I was also able to put all her suggested changes in place in the manuscript. But once again, I was so grateful for Joy's support and for her sensible suggestions.

Some years later, when two Braille copies of *Laura* were produced, I checked if my friend wanted one, which she did. I sent it to her with fear and trembling, but I need not have worried. A few weeks later, she phoned, congratulating me on the novel. She had very much enjoyed it and believed it would truly help sighted people understand issues faced by the visually impaired. And I was delighted that she planned to donate her copy to the only Christian Braille lending library in the US so others could also be blessed.

Around this time, Joy and I had several important conversations about the creative process and its relationship to our faith in God. I was now immersed in my writing, trying to complete the first draft of *Laura* and about to re-write the second part of my original *Heléna*, and had begun to realise the deep spiritual impact all this creativity was having on me. I felt I was noticing people more and valuing them simply for who they were. And my ministry to others seemed to have become more 'organic'—more about relating person to person in the everyday connections of life rather than through any specific church structure. In fact, I found myself a little irked by the inflexibility of some church organisations with whom I was connected and their tendency to put people in a 'box', labelling and thus restricting their ministry at times. My own ministry had no real 'shape' anymore, yet it felt so right and so fulfilling, despite the frustrations I encountered at times.

I was definitely changing and growing in different ways—or as Joy put it, being 'crafted on the inside' even as I crafted my novels. This worried me a little, since I could not quite understand what was happening. Joy helped me see, however, that even though the way I related to God had changed somewhat, it did not mean this was any less valid or less 'spiritual' than anything I had already experienced.

'In fact, everything we've done or experienced in the past feeds into where we find ourselves now, don't you think?' Joy suggested. 'Nothing's wasted—we're "all of a piece"!'

Joy also encouraged me to ask God what these changes in me were all about and to trust my responses. She understood so well how I was feeling, having experienced a similar 'stripping down' in ministry. Everything was changing for her as well, as God seemed to be leading her deeper into her own 'hidden work'. David's illness was affecting her on so many levels too, leaving her with less emotional energy for any substantial output. I tried not to burden her now with too many of my issues, yet she still seemed to want me to come and share what was happening in my life. I sensed I provided a little window to the world outside her family at that time and hoped and prayed any resultant breeze would bring her the refreshment she needed.

I had almost come to the end of my patience with my publisher by this point. I was told my novel had been held up because of the illness of my book title manager, but one by one, each new release date I was given came and went, with no sign of my novel. I had finished *Laura* by now and also completed an extensive revision of what had been the second part of the original *Heléna*, to be entitled *All the Days of My Life*. This had involved my adding new material to the original content so that this sequel would be the same length as my first novel. I had also tried hard to add just enough back story to enable someone who might not have read *Heléna* to make sense of the sequel. I had learnt a lot in the process, but was eager to put these novels behind me and tackle a new challenge.

I suspected I knew already what this new challenge would be. I had wanted for some time to write a story about a girl who believed she was called to go to theological college and become part of the ministry team of a local church. This novel, entitled *Jenna*, would not be my story, I decided, although I would include some of my own experiences in it. My main reason for writing this novel was to encourage women to pursue all God was calling them to do. But my secondary aim was to address the issues still prevalent in some circles of devaluing and refusing to utilise the unique leadership and teaching gifts of women. While I was passionate about these things, I did not want to offend anyone, so was approaching this new novel with some fear and trepidation. And I soon realised there were still vestiges of that little girl who wanted to please everyone inside me.

Joy was also passionate about the themes of this novel and was determined to help me rise to the challenge. In her wisdom, she suggested I try to be less concerned about the outcome of all my novels—particularly this one.

'Do you think you could perhaps let things fall away from you and become a little more detached?' she asked me one day. 'You know, it's not all up to us.'

I knew she was right—and I knew God could be trusted. My task was to be obedient to God's leading and write the best novels I could, then do my utmost to promote them. But I had no control over whether people would respond positively to them or not. And if *Jenna* were to ruffle a few feathers, then so be it.

Towards the end of that year, I attended an amazing weeklong writing course entitled 'Catch the Whisper' that boosted my confidence as an author so much. From the outset, participants were encouraged to let go of any expectations and the need to control. We were told to leave our 'critic'— along with whatever else we had written or were writing—outside the door and instead 'embrace ambiguity'. First off each morning, we received helpful input on a variety of topics such as the use of honest dialogue and incorporating detail into our novels and were then given exercises relating to these areas. However, a large part of each day was spent writing in silence, which we were all urged to respect. At regular intervals, our teacher would speak out three disconnected phrases or 'offerings', at least one of which we were encouraged to accept and include in our writing. Then at the end of each day, we were given an opportunity to share what we had created.

I loved it all. While others struggled with the silence, I revelled in it. I also enjoyed the challenge of accepting the 'offerings' I heard, soon discovering how they fostered much more creativity and lateral thinking in me. As the course unfolded, I felt more and more fulfilled and free and somehow empowered. God was so present to me, I later told Joy, in the silence, in the ideas shared and in the surroundings. God had known what I needed. And I knew without a doubt at the end of that week that I was an author—in fact, a 'born writer', as our teacher told me when we said goodbye.

Christmas came—and still no published first novel. During my first visit to Joy in the new year, she poured herself into encouraging me in my writing of *Jenna* and reminded me to be true to myself in the things I decided to include, rather than always aiming to please others. She was also concerned about my general wellbeing, encouraging me to guard my writing time and to set clear boundaries for family members in this regard. At the same time, she was walking through the middle of a very difficult period in her own life. With David's health declining further, she knew he would soon need to move to the nearby nursing home.

'Each day, I believe I'm learning to understand more of what Jesus meant when he said, "*Blessed are the poor in spirit*",' she told me with such sadness during one visit.

I wished I could have helped her more. I could see and feel her grief—and I upheld her in prayer as she and her family struggled on.

At last, in March of that year (2007) my first novel *Heléna* was released. The most surreal moment for me in it all was not so much holding that initial copy in my hand, but rather seeing the proposed cover for the first time. Some weeks before the novel's release, I opened an attachment on an email from my publisher—and my whole screen was filled with an image of the suggested cover. I could not believe *Heléna* was at last about to come into being, that it was to have such a beautiful cover and—most amazing of all—that my name was on it!

I decided to ask our old church if I could combine the launch of *Heléna* with an event my friend whom I had visited in Turkey was planning to hold there. She had been home in Australia for some months but was about to leave again. She was planning to call the evening 'Destination Turkey' and conceived the idea of setting up half the church as the inside of an aeroplane. Once the people had 'boarded', refreshments would be served and I would provide the 'in flight entertainment' in the form of my book launch! Then we would all 'alight', move to a large floor map of Turkey on the other side of the church and proceed with the Turkish part of the evening.

I was delighted when Joy said she would come and could stay overnight with us—one of her daughters would care for David. When she arrived, she gave me a beautiful candle in a pottery container, decorated with painted sprigs of rosemary and the word 'rosemary' written on it. I smiled to myself. Joy did not know as yet that I had called one of my favourite characters in *Jenna* Rosemary— a wonderful, older woman with a striking resemblance to Joy herself! She also gave me a card on which she had written:

> Dearest Jo-Anne
>
> *What a great day it is! So much work, so much prayer, walking with God, learning all sorts of things and, not least, staying focused and persistent. What a woman! I appreciate and admire and enjoy you so much and join with much joy with your family and friends in congratulating you and your Lord.*
>
> *Much love, Joy*

And as an extra note above this she had also written in large letters: *Keep the light burning!*

I felt I needed to warn her I had dedicated my novel to her, rather than surprise her at the launch itself. She was overcome and unsure whether she had contributed enough to my writing journey to warrant such an honour. During the launch, it was my great delight to present a copy publicly to her and thank her for all she had done for me. And I was also able to keep my promise to my young manuscript reader's family that I had made over a year earlier at her memorial service. The dedication inside my book read:

For Joy Crawford—my 'lifesaver'—and in loving memory of a special young woman, Emily Chapman, 1985-2006.

CHAPTER FOURTEEN

SPEAKING AGAIN

At my book launch, I reminded everyone of something I had said at my farewell over four years earlier. Back then, I had felt God saying: *'Yes, your ministry here was a privilege, Jo-Anne. And I have another wonderful privilege for you down the track—but you might have to wait a while.'* At the time, I had wondered if that new privilege would be writing the novel I had wanted to write for so long. Now, I told them, I knew this was the case. I felt so thankful God had brought this dream of mine to reality. God had seen me through that long waiting period— and Joy had played a big part in that.

But I was beginning to discover there was more to this next 'wonderful privilege' as well. One of the things I had most missed since leaving our church was the opportunity to speak publicly on a regular basis. Not long before my novel was released, however, I sensed God saying: *'Come on, Jo-Anne—time to start speaking again!'* Why I did not see this earlier, I am unsure, as I knew I was required to promote my book myself as much as possible. But now, with blinding clarity,

I realised God was also about to restore to me the very thing I had missed so much.

Soon I began to receive invitations to speak to various groups and also in some services. Needless to say, Joy was delighted God was using me in this way again. I loved all my speaking engagements, despite having to put my writing aside to prepare well for each one. At first, I did not have to look far for invitations. But as time went on, I found I had to network well to find other places to speak and other avenues where I could promote my novel. It was difficult not to feel a little pushy in the process, but in talking with Joy during one visit, I realised my old insecurity problem was trying to rear its head again.

'I guess the worst people can say when I contact them is "Thanks, but no thanks"!' I laughed. 'But in all this, I don't want to rely on my own ability to organise things and lose sight of God.'

That week after driving home, I wrote out a prayer in my journal, expressing how I felt:

'Lord, help me to stay focused on you in all this book business. Help me to know where to go under your leading—I don't want to push to take my books to places I'm not supposed to go. Lord, open up your places for me. And help me to keep the main thing the main thing! May I always remember why I wrote my books—and may I be focused not only on my own success but on lifting you up and enabling people to be drawn to you. Thank you for the open doors you have given me already—what you open, no one can shut.'

I had begun to discover, as I had often heard at writers' festivals and seminars, that writing the book was only the first step. In this day and age, I was told, an author had to have a good platform and must be prepared to speak anywhere and everywhere. I was so thankful God had ensured I had experience in speaking before I embarked on my writing journey. Whereas many authors dread this aspect of their work, I revelled in the opportunity to share not only about my book but also about the things of God wherever I was asked to speak.

During this time, I was still trying to understand the different kind of spirituality emerging in me as a result of my writing journey and discover where I fitted in the local church. I had certainly changed. Now it felt so fulfilling to be able to share my faith in God in a natural way through my writing and also my speaking. The whole process felt much more organic, as I had shared with Joy earlier—it was as if by being 'me', I could achieve what God wanted me to achieve in this world. By this stage, I had become part of a tiny café church in a multicultural neighbourhood not far from our home. My husband was in the midst of another interim ministry, again too far away for me to join him each Sunday. I chose to attend the café church, firstly because it was in an area where many Turkish people lived and secondly because I loved the spirit of the couple who led this church and their heart for God. And I loved how they supported me from their hearts as I served God through my writing and speaking. While they might not have understood fully what I was doing, they trusted and respected me as I endeavoured to travel this different road and be the person God wanted me to be.

Meanwhile, Joy's journey had become even more difficult. Earlier that year, she had faced the necessity of placing David in the nearby nursing home. Her family were all supportive, but she grieved as David's grip on reality became weaker and often wondered if she had done the right thing, letting him go to the nursing home. She knew she could not have coped any longer herself, physically and emotionally, even with the help of home care nurses. But it was a sad, desolate period for her as she spent time with David on an almost daily basis, returning alone after each visit to their large, empty home.

I grieved for her and marvelled at how she still somehow managed to enter into my world whenever I visited. I was even less sure at times now whether to bother her—whether my visits perhaps sapped her of any remaining emotional energy—but she seemed to want me to continue coming. I would share how my writing of *Jenna* was going and any struggles I was having with that. I would regale her with accounts

SOUL FRIEND

of places where I had spoken and comments people had made about my books. And I would read little snippets out to her from my journal and discuss all sorts of issues I was thinking about. Our relationship was still so valuable to me, particularly when I was so much longing for fellowship with other Christians who understood the whole area of creativity and where faith fitted in that.

On one occasion, we delighted together over the title of a brief article about me that had appeared in the alumni magazine of my old university. The title was W*riting for the Soul*.

'I *love* it!' I told Joy. 'I gave them the information for the article, but I didn't give them a title for it. I think it sums up very well what I'm trying to do, don't you? I only hope I can live up to such an exalted calling.'

Joy encouraged me to hold onto that purpose in my writing and also to hold onto myself in the midst of all my writing, promoting and selling.

'God seems to be doing something very special in you,' she commented. 'It's like a "distilling" process—that "stripping away" we talked about some time back.'

I wanted to stay on that journey with God of being able to express the real me in my writing and speaking, sharing God's heart of love and grace with others. I was beginning to feel more at home in my writing, as I came to understand more about the intricacies of crafting a good novel. I could tell I was learning to relax, both in myself and in my writing style—my characters were becoming more real and their conversation less formal and stilted. There was so much still to learn, I knew, but I felt much closer to becoming the writer God had created me to be.

It was hard for me to explain this, even to Joy, but in an indirect way, it was Joy who provided me with the words I needed. We had been talking together one day about simplicity—about listening to God in our lives and following the clear call of love to share the Gospel however we were gifted. In the process, Joy quoted some lines about simplicity from the long poem *Little Gidding* by T S Eliot[32], with which I was unfamiliar. She was unable to find the poem then, but promised to send me a copy as soon as possible.

A few days later, three photocopied pages of the last few stanzas of the poem arrived in the mail. I sat down and read the lines Joy had quoted over again, but then my glance strayed further up the page. For a moment, I sat stunned. My eyes had alighted on some lines that described exactly how I was feeling as far as my writing was concerned.

We shall not cease from exploration
And the end of all our exploring
Will be to arrive where we started
And know the place for the first time.

I doubted that the meaning I saw in those lines was what TS Eliot had intended, but for me, they expressed well the strange sense I had that by choosing to write, I had come full circle in my life and returned to something I had loved way back in the beginning. I needed to go through my many other life experiences, but had now returned to that deep, longstanding desire within me to write. I had not recognised it back in the beginning. I was too young—and besides, being a writer was not something our family would have considered a wise career move. But now it was as if God had opened my eyes to recognise the person I was meant to be and had given me this opportunity to bring to birth all those creative ideas deep inside.

Another issue Joy and I discussed at this time was the term 'Christian fiction'. I had never been comfortable with it, although I found it hard to say why.

'I guess I'd like to think of myself as a writer of novels that bring people closer to God in some way, rather than labelling them "Christian fiction", I told her. 'I'd much prefer to be called a Christian writer of fiction than a writer of Christian fiction, if you understand what I mean. What is "Christian fiction" anyway? If it means using certain vocabulary to do with God and the Bible or fitting some formula or having a particular theological slant, then I don't want to write it. For me, that's too restrictive. I'd like to think God's Spirit shines through everything I write—and I'd like to think anyone, Christian or otherwise, can read and enjoy what I write.'

I also shared with Joy some thoughts I had read on this subject from Madeleine L'Engle's collection of writings, *Glimpses of Grace*.[33]

'L'Engle goes so far as to call it "presumptuous" to declare a particular painting or symphony or book "Christian". She maintains the only way of telling is to see if the work resonates in people's hearts and causes them to live more deeply in God. I guess I might have reservations about some of her comments, but I understand where she's coming from.'

'I suppose it's like the Celtic Christians in one way,' Joy commented in response. 'For them, there was no separation between the sacred and the secular. God was woven throughout all their daily activities and present in all sorts of natural ways. Is that part of what you're saying?'

I nodded. I knew what Joy was referring to—we had often talked about the Celtic way of life and how, for these early Christians, God was present in all things. Joy had travelled to the Isle of Cumbrae off the Scottish coast on several occasions to spend time with the Community of Celebration and the 'Fisherfolk' and share in their simple lifestyle. In the course of these visits, she and David had also travelled to Iona, where the Irish missionary St Columba established a monastery in 536AD and from where Celtic Christianity had spread across Scotland. I had wanted to learn more about these early Christians, so at Joy's suggestion, had read some of the writings of John O'Donohue,[34] J Philip Newell[35] and Esther de Waal[36] on Celtic spirituality and prayer. And Joy was right—I did want to convey in my novels that sense of God's presence every moment of the day, permeating the whole of life, just as the Celtic Christians believed.

In April that year (2008), my second novel *All the Days of My Life* was at last published. I was relieved—I had hated to leave people up in the air so long, wondering what had happened to my character Heléna after she arrived in Australia. At first, it had been a challenge to choose a title for this sequel, but in the end, I opted for the words from Psalm Twenty-Three, already chosen for one of the section dividers in the novel. To me it summed up Heléna's whole attitude—that whatever happened, God would be with her in her new country all the days of her life.

I wanted Joy to be present at my second book launch. This time, I decided to hold a 'Coffee and Dessert' event on a Saturday evening at the little café church I was then attending. The minister and his wife, who worked as baristas in the coffee shop in the church building during the week, offered to make 'proper coffee' for my guests and help with the desserts. Since my husband had to attend another event that afternoon, I myself drove to the mountains to pick up Joy and bring her back to our home for an early tea. I felt privileged to do this for her and to be taking her with me to the launch. Joy helped me set out drinks and nibbles and then we lit a number of candles I had brought from home, since it was Earth Hour that evening.

It was wonderful to watch friends and family arrive. Joy did not know many people, but seemed relaxed as she sat in a comfortable old lounge chair chatting to a good friend of mine. When everyone had arrived, our minister spoke for a brief time. I then shared a few words about the journey I had taken with my book, presented a copy to our two granddaughters, since I had dedicated this novel to my family, and thanked various people for their help, including Joy. Then our minister's wife prayed for God's blessing on the book and on my ministry, which both Joy and I found very moving.

'Why don't you share that little meditation you said when you spoke here last week, Jo?' our minister suggested then.

At first, I was unsure what he meant, but then remembered. It was a special moment as I looked around the candlelit room at all the familiar faces and spoke aloud words I had learnt somewhere in my childhood:

> God is with me now, closer than breathing
> And nearer than hands and feet.
> God has made me for himself.
> I come from God,
> I belong to God,

I go to God.
God knows me,
God loves me,
God has a use for me
Now and forever.
Amen

We then moved into the café itself, returning with our coffee and dessert or finding a spot to sit on the small front balcony. In the process, Joy commented how wonderful it was to hear again the meditation I had shared.

'I've known and loved it for years too,' she told me. 'In fact, I have it in a frame beside my bed. Where did you find it?'

'My mother taught it to me when I was little,' I explained. 'I think she learnt it from a member of the Bush Brotherhood during her years in the Anglican Church in Queensland. I've tried to find out who wrote it but haven't had any success.'

I found it moving that we both loved the same meditation and had known it for so many years. For me, it drew us even closer together and was indicative of the similar ways in which God would often speak to us. And I found it even more interesting when Joy told me she liked to change the word '*use*' at the end of the meditation to '*work*'.

'Somehow the phrase "*God has a use for me*" makes me feel a bit like a commodity,' she told me.

'That's amazing!' I responded, laughing. 'I've always felt the word "*use*" didn't fit well either, but I never thought of changing it.'

Joy had arranged for one of her daughters to pick her up to save me from having to drive her home. I was delighted to meet her daughter and touched to see how far Joy's family would go to ensure she could make it to my launch, especially during a time when they were all so concerned about David's health.

To our great satisfaction, Joy and I often found we loved the same poems or books or authors. During one of my visits at this time, Joy mentioned the book *The Shack* by William Young,[37] which had caused quite a stir in Christian circles and wider afield in recent times. I owned a copy and had read it, so on arriving home, posted it to her. While I had questions about some concepts in the book, I had nevertheless found it a moving and fascinating read and looked forward to discussing it when Joy and I next met.

When I did make it up the mountains again, I was not disappointed. Joy had also been moved and comforted through the book. We had both loved the way Young portrayed the Trinity of Father, Son and Holy Spirit, making a rather difficult concept much more accessible. And we agreed wholeheartedly with one of the book's endorsers where he described *The Shack* as 'a journey to the very heart of God'. We too had felt bathed in the gracious love and mercy of God as we turned its pages.

I then shared with Joy some interesting thoughts and phrases I had noted in the book. I loved how the author chose to describe emotions at one point as being '*the colours of the soul*', which I felt gave them great depth and dignity. I was challenged to look at myself when I read Jesus' words to Mack, the main character, that those who love him are the ones who can live in true freedom, without any agenda. And I was intrigued by the idea expressed during a conversation between God ('Papa' in the book) and Mack that we can never disappoint God because God already knows everything—past, present and future—so has no other expectations of us. All these provided much discussion and food for thought for both of us. But the words I felt were most apt for Joy at that particular time in her life were those the author quoted at one point from the poet Kahlil Gibran—'*Sadness is a wall between two gardens.*'[38] Joy knew the day would come when she would see beyond her wall of sadness over David's illness and his need to be in the nursing home, but for her there was still much pain and grief as she continued to walk the last few months of his journey with him.

Yet despite this great sadness, two days after my visit, I received a beautiful card from Joy, featuring a photo of an old shack high up in the Snowy Mountains in the midst of beautiful snow gums. In it she had written:

Dear Jo-Anne
It was great to talk with you this afternoon, especially about
The Shack*! Thank you for lending it to me. Lots to think*
about. God is wonderful! I will be/am praying for Saturday's
breakfast talk and your input—a great pleasure.
Much love always, Joy.

Another book we discussed together around this time was one
Joy recommended to me—*The Gift of Being Yourself* by American
psychologist and spiritual director David Benner.[39] This book
reminded me yet again of the importance of knowing God's love and
the impact this makes on our preparedness to be who God made us to
be. I identified with many of Benner's insights, especially concerning
our lack of trust that God has our wellbeing at heart and desires to
spend time with us. But above all, Joy and I valued this book for the
way it validated our desire to fulfil our own unique calling in life, to be
that unique image of God we are created to be and reflect God to the
world in a way that fits the 'shape of our being'. I felt I had discovered
that shape through writing, but knew I needed to continue resting in
God's great love for me.

In September that year, I travelled to Turkey for the fifth time to
visit my friend. I was gone for a month, during which time we explored
some amazing and unique places in Turkey before heading back to
Tarsus. Our journey took us from Ankara to Safranbolu, a picturesque,
world heritage listed town with many fine, old, restored Ottoman
houses and on to Amasra on the Black Sea coast. We then headed
inland again to the stately city of Kastamonu and from there in zigzag
fashion back to the Black Sea coast to the old port of Sinop. Next, we
travelled inland yet again to Amasya, a fascinating town surrounded by
mountains and cliffs into which many old tombs were carved centuries
ago. Much to our delight, we were the only guests in an old Ottoman
house overhanging the river. Finally, we headed back to Ankara via
one of the most amazing areas in Turkey—the ancient, world heritage
listed Hittite ruins and rock carvings at Hattuša, near Boğazkale. At

times, we found it hard to grasp we were standing on the ruins of houses build around the fourteenth century BC, possibly pre-dating even Moses.

After I returned, I put together an album of my photos and headed up to see Joy again. Joy was fascinated by the unique places I had visited and interested in all our adventures. In particular, I shared with her how I had stood amongst the Hittite ruins, sensing God's presence at this time in history, yet realising that, thousands of years earlier, people had lived and worked in that same spot. Yes, they had worshipped other gods, but they were still created in the image of the one true God.

'These people must have looked around just as we did at the trees and rocks and the blue sky,' I marvelled. 'It felt so surreal, but it reminded me of God's incredible patience with us human beings down through the centuries. And there we were, so blessed to have come to know Jesus, the Son of God, and to have been called into God's own family.'

Despite her own grief for David, Joy entered into my experiences in this country that had been at the very centre of early Christianity. But it touched me how she was so eager to hear news of my friend in Turkey, too. This friend had stayed in *The Quiet House* for a few days on one occasion and had appreciated Joy's warm hospitality. I had not hesitated in recommending my friend visit her, given the great help Joy had always been to me. Over the years, several other friends of mine had also visited Joy for counsel and prayer and had all come away blessed and affirmed. Some were going through very difficult situations at the time, but Joy welcomed them all and met them at their place of need.

CHAPTER FIFTEEN

CHANGES

All through these months, I had continued to persevere with writing *Jenna*, as well as speaking at a variety of places. I had submitted *Laura* to my publishers, wondering what they would make of this, my third novel. At last, I received the news that it had been accepted for publication and would be released in July the following year. Joy was delighted it would be published, after all my difficulties with the early chapters.

It was now November. I knew David's condition had worsened but did not like to keep contacting Joy to ask what was happening. Then one day she phoned me. David had passed away and his funeral was to be held the following Thursday. As often seems to happen in these moments, I did not know what to say, but my heart went out to her. I could tell, even in this phone call, how shattered she was feeling.

'I'll be at the funeral, Joy,' I told her. 'I'm so sorry—David was a true gentleman.'

The little church at Lawson in the mountains was packed by the time I arrived. I sat towards the back, not knowing anyone, apart from Joy and two of her daughters. From the outset, I sensed all around me a deep love and respect for David and a true desire to honour him as we joined together in what the family had entitled 'a celebration and thanksgiving for the life of David Crawford'. David had loved music, playing the organ and piano himself in some of the churches where he had served, and also good liturgy. In keeping with this, both were reflected well in the service as it unfolded. At one stage, a grandson sang a song he had composed for the occasion and at another, a granddaughter read out a beautiful poem. These, combined with various heartfelt eulogies from friends and family members, showed how David had been loved and valued. A long-time friend of David and Joy's from a small community near Canberra also gave some thoughtful input. This community had grown out of the one David and Joy had been part of years earlier at Malabar, and again, this man's love and respect for David was obvious. Later, we all joined together in reading a beautiful Iona litany, 'Morning Comes', and a prayer Joy had often prayed with David during the last days of his illness, written by J Philip Newell, Warden of Iona Abbey.

Most moving of all for me, however, was the moment when David and Joy's four daughters, along with other family members, carried his coffin down the aisle at the conclusion of the service, singing a simple worship song they had often sung together. Here was a person who had been loved and respected by his family and had stood for God and for what he believed throughout his life. As I left the church, I decided I would love to be farewelled in that way, too. Yet would my family be willing to carry my coffin, singing as they went, as David's daughters had?

I did not go to the nearby cemetery for the short committal service, but waited at the church hall along with others for the family's return. I felt it would be presumptuous to intrude on such a personal time intended for family and close friends. Later, however, Joy asked me if I had been at the committal and was disappointed I had not felt free to do so. Her response showed she considered me a close friend, which touched me.

During the Christmas and New Year period following David's death, I phoned Joy, although not often. Again I felt a little intrusive—this was a time of deep grieving for her. But, as the weeks went by, I contacted her a little more often and at last arranged to visit her again. I decided my visit would be brief—I felt I needed to care for her at this point and did not want to burden her with any mundane issues of mine. I took with me some homemade biscuits I knew she liked—small Turkish cookies baked to a simple recipe and tasting like shortbread—and some Anzac biscuits. We enjoyed our morning tea together, but Joy's tiredness and grief were obvious and my heart went out to her. Yet she still seemed to want to hear what was happening in my life and, in particular, how my novel *Jenna* was progressing.

In actual fact, it had progressed quite slowly. Yet I could not complain, since this was due in part at least to the increased number of speaking engagements I had that year. But another factor that had changed things for me was that my husband was now semi-retired and therefore no longer in ministry at a specific church. This brought with it a different daily routine at home for both of us and also meant we needed to find a church to attend together again. We tried several, finally choosing one where we knew the senior pastor well. But this was not an easy decision for me. The further I went in my writing journey, the less comfortable I felt as I tried to participate in the life of a normal, structured, contemporary church.

It was difficult to talk about such things with my close friends and family, many of whom were happy at the churches they attended. Besides, they had not travelled the same writing journey I had—how could they be expected to understand fully? Again, however, despite her great loss, Joy managed to come to my rescue. Again, she understood and was prepared to listen to my struggles and fears about becoming an integral part of another local church.

Part of the reason Joy understood was that she herself had

experienced similar feelings. All through their years of local church ministry, she and David had been at the forefront of introducing innovative approaches to worship and to 'doing' church. In particular, their last ministry at Surry Hills had involved trialling new ways of caring for street people and reaching out to them in Jesus' name. But since David's retirement, Joy had struggled to find a local church where she felt comfortable. She had kept searching, regularly attending a local, informal gathering of Christians nearby who sought to follow the leading of God's Spirit and do things somewhat differently. She also participated in several local small groups at different points, including a Christian meditation group and others studying a particular book or course. As well, the times of silent worship with David and others in their own tiny chapel each week had also fed her spirit. This was one thing I valued so much about Joy—she was always seeking to grow and look for new ways of worshipping and walking with God, of sharing with other Christians and of living out the Gospel in everyday life in an authentic manner.

I also discussed with Joy some things I was grappling with in books about the 'emerging church' I had read. I had been challenged by several confronting statements in George Barna's and Frank Viola's book *Pagan Christianity?*,[40] which asserted that much of what we do in church is rooted in pagan culture rather than in the New Testament. I was unsure about some of Viola's ideas in his book *Re-imagining Church*,[41] wondering if they would work. I had been intrigued enough by its title to read Jacobsen's and Coleman's book *So You Don't Want To Go To Church Anymore*.[42] And I was also trying to come to grips with Michael Frost's comprehensive and at times provocative book *Exiles*,[43] encouraging us to lead 'missional' lives in the midst of what is now a post-Christian culture and to rediscover a 'robust, poetic' faith. I wondered if some of his claims were overstated, however. I was unsure, for example, whether the church in general had made the gospel uninteresting, 'shapeless' and inane, as he asserted—I even felt a little angry and defensive at such statements. Yet I also found myself in agreement with much of what he said and it was a relief to share these conflicting emotions with Joy.

Not long after this, I met with the senior minister of the church we were now attending to discuss church involvement with him. As we talked, I felt God showed me that the main issue for me was fear—in particular, the fear of being asked to do various types of church-related ministry again and of seeing needs I knew I could meet, resulting in my having little time to write.

'I guess the question is whether I see my writing as an equally legitimate ministry, isn't it?' I commented to Joy when I next visited her and told her about the meeting. 'I think I do, but our minister pointed out that if I wasn't involved in the life of the church, I would be missing out not only on receiving from others but also giving to them.'

'Of *course* what you do is a legitimate ministry!' Joy said in an indignant voice. 'I think it's *wonderful*—you give out to all sorts of people, in and outside the church. It's not inferior at all.'

I was so grateful to her for her firm response. I still needed such reassurance at times to continue to believe that what I was trying to achieve through my writing and speaking was a valid ministry. Yet whether others saw it that way or not, it was what God had called me to do. I knew, as Joy had quoted to me from a favourite poem earlier on in my writing journey, that God was still saying, '*I have need of you, free*'. Yes, linked into a local church, but not so involved with ministry there that I could not be free to write and to speak elsewhere.

Already I was seeing the value of being free and available to be used by God in different settings. I had begun to find interesting and natural ways of being 'salt and light' in our community through my writing and speaking. The first involved the simple act of giving one of my novels to our neighbours and chatting with them in the process. What resulted from that was a much warmer relationship with each family and even requests for more books.

My second new way of reaching out came through the Living Library program at a local library, a scheme whereby members of the community would 'borrow' people instead of books to talk to for twenty minutes at a time. I called my book 'My Writing Journey' and was often 'borrowed' whenever the Living Library functioned. Through this, I was able to talk with a diverse group of 'readers' from a variety of ethnic backgrounds and faiths and was often able to mention my faith in God as I described what my books were about.

My third way of touching others' lives came about through being invited to speak to some secular groups. My journey in this area had only begun, but already I had discovered what an amazing privilege it was to be able to speak about my writing journey to seniors' groups in our own local shopping centre's community room and to other similar groups.

My fourth new way of being 'salt and light' was a little different. One day I happened to see a writing workshop advertised through the NSW Writing Centre called 'Writing as Religious Practice'. It intrigued me, as at that time I was still thinking through how the creative act of writing influenced my faith in God and vice versa. Because I was busy, I decided against attending at first. But then it occurred to me that a workshop on 'Writing as Religious Practice' was the very place where Christian authors should be found, so I changed my mind. This turned out to be an excellent day of writing and reflection, interspersed with readings from works by the American poet Mary Oliver. The fact that the lecturer was a practising Buddhist soon became clear, but I also noticed she used the technique of focusing as a means of helping us 'centre down' before writing. At the end of the day, I was able to talk with her about this and share how I used focusing in the context of prayer and listening to God. I came away from that Sunday sensing it had been God's will for me to be there, not only to share with the lecturer but also to add a Christian 'flavour' to our group discussions.

Joy was delighted with these diverse opportunities to speak and share in secular settings, and encouraged me to keep pursuing such openings. Sometimes we would talk about the fact that God was present wherever I was speaking—so was there as definite a divide as we might think between the 'sacred' and the 'secular'? I had been amazed at how much I was able to say about God in these non-church settings, without seeming to offend anyone. And even when I did not get any opportunity to do this, I felt my presence at these events and the conversations I had still made a difference. Even by answering questions about writing in a helpful, patient way or listening with empathy to someone's story or praying silently for the people I met, I felt I was bearing witness to God in that place.

I wished I could have spent more time with Joy as she continued to travel through this period of mourning. I knew I had to focus on my busy speaking schedule, however, and try to continue my writing in the midst of it all. I smiled at times when I looked at the list of places where I had been invited to speak—two women's weekend retreats; morning services in churches of various denominations, ranging from traditional and conservative to contemporary and relaxed; a Probus (Senior Rotary) meeting at a local RSL Club; a Christian Librarians' Conference; a school; a secular seniors' club; a women's coffee night at a church. I viewed it all as a great privilege and was so thankful that, by God's grace, my background and life experiences had equipped me to speak with sensitivity but also confidence in different settings and denominations.

I had also learnt something else by this stage, however. A few months earlier, a Christian friend suggested I needed a prayer team to support me in all my speaking engagements and offered to be its first member. I thought about it for a while. I was not a missionary or an important church leader, yet I knew I could not and should not do this ministry unsupported. While it was enjoyable, it could also be challenging and tiring at times. So, despite my reluctance to ask for such support, I began praying about which friends I should approach. I knew I had to restrict my potential prayer team to those with email access—and also those who checked their emails often. In the end, I found nine wonderful women willing to be contacted in this way and to pray.

One of the first I asked was Joy. She agreed at once and seemed delighted to be part of it. Soon after forming the team, I began to send out an email entitled 'My next adventure' a few days before I spoke somewhere. Afterwards, I would send a report, often including the details of my next 'adventure' as well. In the early months of the team's existence, Joy would often reply to my prayer emails with a few brief, encouraging words and seemed to appreciate being kept up to date. But now, in the midst of her grief, I wondered if my emails were becoming a burden to her.

'I seem to be sending so many emails to my prayer team lately,' I told her. 'I don't want to bother you with all my requests right now, so please don't feel you have to read them or pray.'

'Oh no,' she assured me, 'I love knowing what you're doing and I appreciate the little reports you send afterwards.'

Even during this sad, 'lost' time, Joy did her best to support me. In August that year (2009), my novel *Laura* was released. I decided to hold my book launch on a Sunday afternoon. Both Joy and I had hoped she would be able to attend, particularly because she also knew my friend who had inspired this novel. However, after the date was set, I discovered she had agreed to speak herself that afternoon at the local Christian gathering she often attended. While I was disappointed, I was nevertheless delighted she felt able to share in such a way again— her first time of speaking since David's death. I put a copy of *Laura* aside for her and, soon after, arranged to visit her again. I knew how eager she was to read the book, but I also wanted to check how she was doing.

Joy's family were very supportive, making sure she was not alone too much and looking after her in so many ways. Two of her daughters lived close by and also a much loved granddaughter, while her two other daughters often stayed with her on weekends. Around this time, a villa came onto the market not far from Joy's home and close to where one of her daughters lived. While the family encouraged Joy to consider the move, they wisely left her to make her own decision. As it turned out, she decided not to sell at that point—it simply seemed too much for her, she later told me. She was also not quite ready to leave the home she and David had shared for so long—or their beautiful garden. In the end, one of her daughters rented out her home in Sydney and came to live in *The Quiet House*, working part-time and also studying. This way, Joy had someone nearby most of the time but could also enjoy her own space, as well her beloved garden.

I was so impressed with the loving way Joy's family rallied around her. At one stage, Joy's granddaughter brought her baby son around regularly to be minded by his great-grandmother for a brief time— such a precious, life-giving experience for Joy in the midst of her grief. Sometimes her daughters took her interstate to visit relatives, while each week they held a family gathering in one of their homes nearby. This was a good reminder to me to interact with our own children on a more regular basis and make an effort to stay connected in caring and imaginative ways in the midst of our busy lives.

I also admired the way Joy continued loving and supporting her children and grandchildren in whatever they were doing. I could see each one was close to her heart and that she accepted them equally and prayed for them all. At one stage, Joy shared with me about a beloved grandson who was heading overseas to further his singing career and how she was a little concerned for him and how his future would unfold.

'Always remember you are loved!' she said then with a sigh. 'That's what we have always told our grandchildren and other family members when they head overseas.'

For Joy, that was indeed a foundational belief, that wherever we are in our relationship with God, we are each so loved. I knew she was referring to the love of family as well, but over the years, I had seen that however grieved she was, she always sought to remind herself that God was still there, loving her and holding her close, and would continue to do so. Many times as we had talked together, I had felt so loved, not only by Joy, with her warm, caring manner, but also by God.

But that day, as I left with the phrase *'Always remember you are loved'* ringing in my ears, I found myself more determined than ever to accept God's amazing love for me and to live each day in the light of it.

I also admired the way Joy seemed to accept her children's and grandchildren's need to explore new horizons, making radical choices at times, and how she strove to understand their motives for doing so. I had seen in her that same desire to try new things and to search for a greater understanding of God, of herself and of the world around her, and this had always spurred me on, making me determined never to become stagnant and narrow in my faith. In her earlier ministry years, both alongside David and in her own right, Joy had often been prepared to push the boundaries and seek radical ways of using her gifts to express her love for God. On one occasion when we met, she shared with me a poem she had written in 1992 during a significant three-week personal retreat she undertook:

I saw the power pole break loose
　　as the lurching Melbourne tram
　　rounded a corner,
bouncing here and there in frantic
　　searching for connection,
　　almost joyous dancing,
tram still moving forward
　　on some stored energy within
　　like a chook
yet running after severing of its head,
　　with clanging bell, and
　　someone races out and
guides the flailing thing back
　　to its wire overhead,
　　makes new connection,
a moment's freedom brought to
　　military end, well back in line
　　on those metallic tracks, prescribed.

A tug pulls at my heart
  some deep and yearning place inside
  some hint
that wants to leap strictures
  of culture and convention,
  test the possibilities,
ask the question
  What would I be like
  if I were free?
And then is drowned in tooting horn
  Cries of 'get on with it',
  bustling traffic of life and duty,
  timetables and destinations.
But I did see it, that loose dancing pole,
  for one brief moment in Flinders Street
  I did see it!
And somewhere it reminds me I am
  not connected to something so prescribed
  I am not free,
but to love and life and dancing,
  to that deep darkly planted
  longing to belong,
  be one with all that is
  Creation,
  God,
  myself.

I loved this poem as soon as Joy read it out to me and related to it easily. After all, I had chosen some unusual paths in my own life over the years, rather than head down any prescribed track. Believing God had called me to do so, I had undertaken ministry training in my late forties. I believed in supporting both women and men in ministry and that this was consistent with Scripture. And now I had embarked on what I often termed 'this crazy writing journey of mine', where I had to take risks and face possible rejection, but where I had also tasted that freedom Joy had written about in her beautiful poem. And I marvelled again that God had brought into my life someone as gifted as Joy who understood me and the journey on which I had embarked.

Chapter Sixteen

Celebrations

As Christmas approached, I began to feel very tired. During the course of that year, I had spoken over thirty times, my third novel had been released, my fourth, *Jenna*, had at last been submitted for publication and I was now well into writing my fifth. I toyed with the idea of having a sabbatical in the coming year, free from speaking, when I could regroup a little, complete my current novel and perhaps write another book that had been on my heart for a while. But I had already committed myself to some speaking engagements and felt I could not back out. Besides, while my books were available in Christian bookstores, I knew I needed to do my best to continue promoting them myself.

I was grateful that all my prayer team members had agreed to continue supporting me for another year. Some often emailed encouraging comments after I requested prayer for my latest 'adventure' and Joy was still among them. Some also commented on my weekly blogs, which I had begun writing in the middle of that year, and again Joy was among those. Just at this point when I felt so tired and in need of encouragement, she wrote:

> *Hello, Jo-Anne. Lovely to get your email just now. I'll be praying for that strictly twenty minutes on Saturday!* (I had asked the team to pray my talk would be the right length.)
> *I found your blog today so helpful and to the point. Surely your ministry has the Lord's blessing. Much love, Joy.*

Joy's words not only spurred me on, but also made me feel so blessed that I had encouraged her in some small way.

On the last day of the year, with Joy's encouraging words in mind and having read the first few verses of Luke 5, I committed myself once more to the tasks ahead in the new year and wrote the following in my journal:

> *Simon answered: 'Master, we've worked hard all night and haven't caught anything. But because you say so, I will let down the nets.'*
> *Lord, because you say so, I will 'let down the nets' for another year with my books. I will put myself and my writing out there so others can hear and turn to you. And you are the one who gives the results, just as Luke 5 shows.*

Soon I was again in the throes of writing and speaking. I found myself preparing for an interesting variety of engagements, including a coffee and dessert evening, a seniors' luncheon at a church just up the road from our home, a women's conference, two church 'Couples and Friends' clubs and several engagements at secular seniors' clubs. But I could feel a level of tension inside me I did not like and was concerned I was perhaps trying to be too much in control of everything myself, rather than letting God lead and empower me. Yet, with all my heart, I wanted my writing and speaking to flow from God's heart through me to others. Around that time, I read in John 15 how we can do nothing apart from God. If I attempted things in my own strength, all my busyness would not produce anything worthwhile. Yet, as John 15:16 reminded me, God had called me that day in Turkey when I was reading Isaiah 42 and had chosen me to '*go and bear fruit—fruit that will last*'. And as Joy had written, surely my ministry had the Lord's blessing.

Early in the year, I managed to find time to drive up the mountains to see Joy again. It was still such a wonderful privilege to do this in the midst of all that was happening in my life. And this day, apart from wanting to see firsthand how she was faring, I had some good news to share with her.

'Joy—I can't believe it, but I received an email from my publisher yesterday. They've agreed to publish *Jenna*!' I burst out as soon as we had sat down.

Joy was so delighted. She had continued to pray for this book in particular and had followed my journey with it, believing it was important 'for the Kingdom'. I felt this novel was my best so far, but had been unsure whether my publisher would want to release a story about a girl who trains for ministry. I was therefore relieved and excited that this novel would see the light of day.

'And I have something to ask you, Joy,' I went on. 'I'd love to use your poem "*You ask a drink of me, a woman*" at the front of the book—would that be okay? Of course, I'd acknowledge you wrote it.'

Joy seemed happy to allow me to use her poem, although I sensed she was a little overwhelmed it would be published in this way. Later in the year, as I was putting in place some corrections my publisher wanted me to make, I noticed they had suggested a change to one line of Joy's poem. I was horrified and contacted them straight away, refusing to change anything in the poem. Yet when I emailed Joy about it, she told me she did not mind at all. '*I am not at all upset about it, just sorry you had the worry. Actually, I think it's a bit funny—hilarious, really! I so pray it will all come out well for the Kingdom. That's what matters, isn't it?*' she wrote. This response was Joy to a tee—gracious and humble, with a wonderful sense of humour, but also desiring whatever was best for God's Kingdom.

For some time after that, my visits to Joy became a little sparse because of my busy schedule, but she understood. On one occasion she wrote: *It will be great to see you, but only when you have time. Meanwhile, you are close as I pray for you often.* We stayed in touch by phone and email, but for me, there was nothing like meeting face to face. After one of my rare visits in those months, I emailed her some quotes and a poem I thought she would like and received the following response:

> *Very dear Jo-Anne*
>
> *Lovely to receive your email yesterday. Yes, it was so good to be with you and to share so much. No, I wasn't tired, just blessed and grateful. I was thinking of the book* Anam Cara— *that that was what was happening for each other ...*
>
> *Much love and blessing. Joy*

I was humbled by this gracious email and so glad Joy had experienced something at least of the same blessing I had received as we met. And I knew what she meant by her reference to *Anam Cara*. It was the title of a book on Celtic spirituality by John O'Donohue that we had both enjoyed. The words were from the Gaelic language, I remembered, and meant 'soul friend'. I loved that concept even more than 'spiritual friend' or 'spiritual companion'. To me it spoke of a deep, tender relationship of mutual love and understanding—a relationship of grace and respect where questions could be asked and souls bared. I reflected then how rare such relationships seem to be, even in the body of Christ, and like Joy, felt so blessed and grateful.

As I waited for the publication of *Jenna*, I continued speaking and also writing my fifth novel, *Heléna's Legacy*, which I managed to complete around the middle of that year. But then I was faced with a dilemma. Should I even think about starting a sixth novel? Part of me wanted to—the title and the first chapter were already clear in my head. But another part of me was loath to dive into writing yet again. Did my reluctance mean God was saying I had written enough? Or was this a ploy of the enemy to stop me doing what God wanted? Perhaps it was neither—my mind was so confused. Therefore, when

I saw an advertisement from our own denomination promoting a spiritual retreat, I was interested at once. Here was an opportunity to go away for three days, spend time alone with God, but also join in some small group sessions with other women. Perhaps this was what I needed to sort out the way ahead and to get rid of my tiredness and frustration. I told Joy about it and she was glad I could avail myself of this opportunity.

I enjoyed relating with the other women at the retreat and sharing what was happening for me. And I found it helpful to spend time alone with God. I checked through my journal to remind myself how God had led me thus far, read Scripture and tried to listen to what God might want to say. One day, I walked through nearby bushland and sat beside some beautiful rock pools at the base of a waterfall. I felt God's presence and peace as I contemplated the vast diversity in nature around me, but even this experience did not seem to reach into the very depth of my being. What was wrong? Was I expecting too much?

It was almost time to return for our final evening together. As I made my way back, I felt a sense of disappointment inside which was rapidly turning to self-blame. If I could not hear God, it must be my fault—not God's.

After dinner, we were told we would be enjoying a relaxing night, chatting and eating chocolate as we coloured in together. I was unsure I had heard correctly, but there on a low table were mounds of coloured pencils and felt pens and a pile of papers with intricate patterns on them. We were invited to choose as many or as few patterns as we liked and colour in to our heart's content.

I felt angry and embarrassed. What a childish exercise! Imagine wasting a whole, precious night colouring in! I felt it would be rude not to join in, however, as I watched the others eagerly begin. I looked through the remaining patterns with resignation. Only one caught my eye that I felt was worth colouring in—it was made up of interwoven lines forming four large knots, each connected to the other in an intricate, square pattern. It seemed to have a Celtic feel about it and

I thought of Joy. We both enjoyed the depth and interwoven nature of Celtic spirituality—perhaps I could think about that as I coloured in.

I selected several felt pens in different shades of purple, my favourite colour. If I had to take part in this exercise, my effort would at least be colour coordinated and tasteful. I began to fill in my pattern. I would do the outer edge in a rich, vibrant purple, I decided, then use a lighter purple for one of the interweaving threads. But I soon discovered that, try as I might, I could not find a spot where the thread I was following ended. On and on it went, snaking its way from the outside edge in towards the centre, across to the opposite knot, then out again. I continued on, wishing I could change to my pretty, lighter shade of purple, but was forced to keep going. On and on I coloured, my deep purple thread tricking me at every turn, leading me on a never-ending dance.

At last I realised the design was in fact an endless, interwoven thread or ribbon. I could not change colours anywhere or the pattern would be ruined. I persevered, realising the others were almost finished. In defiance, I used a deep pink to add a few final touches of colour to the background where it peeked through the knots in the design, before returning my unused purple pens to the pile. I knew now what God was saying and felt quite emotional. I decided to hold off when our group leader asked us to share anything God had shown us as we coloured in. But in the end, I decided I at least needed to explain why my pattern was almost completely the one colour.

'When I realised there was nowhere to change colour and still be true to the pattern, I felt so angry and "ripped off",' I told them. 'I wanted to use *all* the beautiful purples I'd chosen—not just one! But I began to realise God was trying to show me something. Then I remembered I verse I read yesterday from Colossians: *Tell Archippus: 'See to it that you complete the work you have received in the Lord.'* So ... I'm sure God was saying I have to stay on this writing path I'm on and complete the work I've been called to do. After I got over my initial anger, I began to feel so relieved I could still hear God.'

There was an awed silence as everyone realised how God had spoken to me. I felt humbled and could not hold back the tears.

When I next caught up with Joy, I showed her the design I had coloured in and told her what had happened. She was amazed and touched.

'It's just like God, isn't it, to use a simple thing like colouring in that I thought was so stupid to teach me a big lesson?' I laughed.

In August that year (2010), I was again invited to speak at our old church in the morning service. I had decided I would not hold a launch for my fourth novel, *Jenna*, but as things unfolded, I realised our old church was a fitting place to celebrate its release. This was where I had been on team—and the novel had certainly been fuelled by my experiences during that time. We would stay after the service and chat over morning tea, I decided, as well as sell my books. Then we would have a celebratory lunch at home for family and close friends.

Of course I wanted Joy to be at the church for the launch and also join us for lunch afterwards. We arranged to drive up the mountains on the Saturday afternoon and have her stay overnight with us, which Joy seemed delighted to do. However, I felt a little nervous, since, apart from my graduation speech and the few words I had said at my first two book launches, Joy had never heard me speak before. I hoped she would enjoy my sermon and did not want to disappoint her. I chose to speak from Romans 12 and entitled my message 'Honouring God with all that I am'. I wanted to remind everyone that each of us is unique, that we have been created in God's image and that we are called to allow this image of God to shine through us to bless others.

It was a delight to introduce *Jenna* to the congregation and point out Joy's poem '*You ask a drink of me a woman*' in the book. And it was an added delight to be able to thank her publicly for allowing me to use it and also for her ongoing support throughout the writing of this novel. I also pointed out how my character Rosemary, Jenna's mentor, was modelled on Joy and that Rosemary made many statements that Joy had said to me over the years. I had tried to portray her as gracious and hospitable, with the wisdom and spiritual insight I knew Joy had, and intended her to be a fitting tribute to Joy and her impact on my life. But I also hoped that as my readers came to appreciate Rosemary and take in her wise counsel to Jenna, so they too would be encouraged.

At home, I found it heart-warming to see Joy sitting with my other friends and family around our table as we shared our celebration lunch together. She looked a little tired, but seemed to be enjoying herself. I noticed in particular how well she related to our younger daughter who was cutting the wonderful chocolate cake she had made for the occasion. Joy loved the fresh lavender flowers placed around the lavender cream that accompanied each slice and with a smile, tucked a flower in her buttonhole.

A little later, I drove her back home up the mountains. She had not wanted to trouble me, but again it was a pleasure to do this for her. As we drove, it was wonderful to de-brief with her about the day and listen to her observations about the service and the people she had met. And when I arrived home again, I read the special card she had given me to mark the launch of *Jenna*. On the front was a rainforest scene with a stream running through it, forming small waterfalls as it flowed over some rocks. The scene reminded me of the Leura Cascades where I had sat so many years earlier, trying to come to grips with the possibility of leaving our ministry team. Now I was at a very different place in my life—and Joy had been such a large part of that transition. Inside the card, she had written:

> Dearest Jo-Anne
>
> Congratulations once more on this fourth launch. I await reading this new book with eager anticipation, and pray a blessing for each copy to **be** a blessing.
>
> May Christ's light shine on through you and in you and your sharing of His life and love wherever He takes you.
>
> With love always, Joy.

Around three weeks later, I received a phone call from her. She had just finished reading *Jenna* and wanted to let me know how much she had loved it.

'It was just beautiful,' she told me. 'So human—but so godly at the same time.'

I was thankful she had enjoyed it. But most encouraging of all was her final comment.

'I loved all your other books,' she went on, 'but I think this is your best yet.'

I had hoped my writing was improving as I relaxed and let the story flow more freely. I had also sensed my characters were becoming more rounded and 'human', as Joy put it. But it was reassuring to have someone else recognise this—particularly when that someone else happened to be Joy.

I was still learning so much from her every time we talked, yet she always maintained our learning was mutual. I had been unable to see this earlier on, but as our relationship continued, I become a little more aware of it through emails Joy sent on occasions. While she was not fully at home in using her computer at that point, she persevered, and emailed me one day after finding some of my blogs online:

> Dear Jo-Anne
>
> I've just spent a very relaxed and happy half hour at least, browsing through your blog and being so blessed and reminded and ministered to by your so beautifully written and apt reflections. Thank you, dear friend, and thank you Lord.
>
> Much love and prayers, Joy.

I was humbled and so encouraged yet again. I had been wondering if all the effort I put into writing my blogs was worthwhile, given the fact I was trying to complete my next novel. Now I realised that even if my blogs ministered to Joy alone, my time writing them had been well spent.

Apart from my regular brief reports to my prayer team members, which still included Joy, I also tried to phone or email her from time to time to see how she was faring as she continued working through her loneliness and grief. On one occasion, I received the following reply:

Very dear Jo-Anne
Thanks so much for your lovely and loving email and for your
prayers. So much to be thankful for and enjoy remembering,
along with times of great sadness that creep up unawares
out of the blue, so to speak, and just have to be lived through,
something like rain when the sun is shining—or not. It
will be great to see you when that's possible. Meanwhile,
I so appreciate receiving info about your doings and the
feedback. You're so good at that. Helps to keep me faithful!
Go gently, much love, Joy.

I also thought of her often at this time, as I knew she had some big decisions to make, including whether to sell her beautiful, old home at last. She felt more able now to make this difficult decision, yet the thought was still daunting for her.

One day she emailed me to ask for prayer for herself. *Dear Jo-Anne,* she wrote, *after much deliberation I have decided to put our house on the market, hoping to buy a villa near our daughter ... I would so value your prayer, dear friend, for a good outcome. ... I feel it is time to make a start on moving anyway.*

I loved the thought of supporting Joy in prayer over this important issue. It was the least I could do, in the light of the many prayers she had prayed over the years on my behalf.

It was now November and I was due to head north to Brisbane to present a workshop at a writers' conference. Just before we left, Joy phoned, inviting me to attend her eightieth birthday party that her family had arranged for her. It was to be held on the following Saturday—the day of my workshop. I was touched that she wanted me there and deeply disappointed I could not accept her invitation, but Joy understood. Later, she emailed to thank me for the gift I sent and tell me about the '*lovely, gentle time of songs, poems, readings, and scrumptious food*' they had enjoyed together. Joy's party sounded just like the kind of celebration I would have expected her to enjoy. I was so happy for her and thankful her ever creative and loving family had rallied round to make her day so memorable.

And so we ministered to each other—but from my perspective, the scales were still very much weighted in my favour.

CHAPTER SEVENTEEN

DECISIONS

Not long before Christmas, Joy phoned to tell me her house had sold within a few days of coming onto the market. I could tell she was still somewhat in shock—it was almost as if she had trouble believing it. She was thankful the whole process had not been prolonged, but also a little panicked at the thought of having to be ready to move out in a few short weeks.

'The family's been wonderful,' she told me. 'They're helping in all sorts of ways. And I've been able to buy the villa I wanted not far from here, just up the street from our daughter.'

I was happy for her, but I also knew how sad she would be to say goodbye to her precious, old home where so many significant events had taken place and where so many memories of David surrounded her. And even as she gave me the news, I felt a pang of grief myself. Much had happened for me there as well since I had first begun see Joy in my second year at college. I had talked and cried my way through so many deep issues in her little study that became a safe haven for me in a sea of new experiences and challenges over the years. I had grown so much and was now more at home with myself as a person. But I still liked the idea of being able to visit that cosy study again whenever I wanted and sit with Joy in God's presence. I needed to visit her before she moved, I decided, not only to see how she was but also to say goodbye to her home myself.

'Please do come up, Jo-Anne,' Joy responded when I mentioned the possibility, 'but only if you have time. Is there anything of mine you'd like to have—perhaps some books? I have so many and there won't be room for them all in my new place.'

I thanked her, but declined the offer. How could I even think of taking any of Joy's books? Besides, I knew the ones I would like were also her favourites—I could not do that to her.

It felt strange to be walking up Joy's driveway for the last time. I gazed at the beautiful, old shrubs and trees in the garden and at the purple clematis and other flowering plants bordering the front deck as I paused for a moment before ringing the doorbell. I wanted to savour the moment and remember the long journey I had taken since I had first stood in that spot and rung that bell.

Then Joy was there, greeting me in her usual warm manner. We made our way past David's huge, old grandfather clock in the hall and on into the kitchen, where Joy had already begun preparing our tray of Lady Grey tea and biscuits.

'Where would you like to sit?' she asked me. 'We can go to the study or out to *The Quiet House*. Or perhaps you'd like to sit on the back porch with me and look out over the garden. You pick!'

For once, I chose the back porch. It seemed such a comfortable place to sit for our last time together there. Besides, I loved her cottage garden, with its interesting mix of plants and shrubs. Joy would miss it, I knew, although she told me how she planned to have a small garden at her new home. As we chatted, she pointed out several plants friends had given her over the years, which continued to remind her of them.

'Perhaps you can take some of them with you, Joy,' I suggested, feeling sad for her.

I was sure Joy and her family would have thought of this already, but she smiled and nodded. We talked on, remembering the different experiences we had shared over the years. The prayer ministry school, my college graduation, the difficult times in ministry when I had relied so much on her support, the spiritual direction conferences we both enjoyed, our wonderful Beethoven concert at the Opera House, my book launches—and also David's passing. God had been so faithful, carrying us through it all, comforting us, encouraging us, rejoicing with us and never, ever leaving us alone.

And now Joy was facing another whole new phase of her life. As I sat enjoying the warm summer breeze and trying to sense what God might have me say to her, an old poem that had stood on our dining room sideboard when I was a child came to mind.

'Joy, I'm remembering a poem my mother used to like when I was young,' I told her. 'It began with the words, "*I said to the man who stood at the gate of the year*".[44] Do you know it?'

She did, but like me could not remember it all. I shared what lines I remembered, especially the last few about putting our hand in God's hand which was '*better than light and safer than a known way*'. I promised I would try to find the poem and send it to her—I wanted to help in any way I could. We prayed together and then set off on a final stroll around the grounds.

We walked past the little fishpond near the back door, across to *The Quiet House* and on into the garden beyond. Here I remembered how Joy had grown a large variety of vegetables and flowers, while in another grassy spot, her granddaughter had been married. Then we made our way to the tiny chapel at the rear of the property. Joy opened the door and I went in, admiring as I did the beautiful stained glass window on one wall. This simple chapel, built by David with such care, was sparsely furnished, with chairs in each corner, a cross at the centre and small icons dotted here and there.

'We've excluded the chapel from the sale,' Joy told me. 'I decided I'd like to put it up somewhere else, if possible. A group of friends from Malabar and some of the family are going to dismantle it soon. But is there anything here you'd like? I won't have room for these old chairs at my new place, for example.'

I glanced around, shaking my head. We went to leave—and then the thought came that I could perhaps use one of the chairs in my own study. Perhaps it would fit in the small space between my desk and the bookshelves. Feeling as if I were stealing something special from Joy, I picked one up.

'Well, perhaps I could take this one for my study—that's if I can fit it in the car. But are you sure that's okay?'

'Absolutely!' Joy reassured me. 'I'd be delighted. That one used to belong to my mother—it's very old and, as you can see, I put a new covering on it at one stage. It needs more fixing up, but if you can use it, that would be wonderful!'

At once we knew we had found the one thing belonging to her I was meant to take. We stood in that little chapel hugging each other with full hearts. Joy was so happy she could give me something, while I felt so blessed to have such a tangible reminder of our times together.

I carried the chair to the car, but found it would not fit in the boot, whichever way I manoeuvred it. As a last resort, I tried sliding it onto the back seat where, to my surprise, it fitted perfectly. And when I arrived home and placed it next to my desk, somehow it looked as if it was meant to be there. The chair had a dark wooden frame, with a back that tilted, and was covered in creamy beige, velvet-like material. Already I was envisaging the girls I mentored sitting in that self-same chair as I passed onto them many of the things Joy had taught me.

That afternoon, I searched for the poem I had shared with Joy and emailed it to her as promised. A few hours later, I received the following response:

Thank you so much for coming today, Jo-Anne. It was so special to sit on the veranda and remember gently and

joyfully so, so many things. Such a time of thankfulness for
me and healing.
Thank you for the poem. Just the one for such a time as this
in my life! God is amazing. And so glad you have the funny
old chair.
Much love, Joy.

I had not known what to say to Joy that would comfort her as she faced moving, but God had undertaken, encouraging us both in the process. And whenever I glanced at the chair beside my desk, I was reminded not only of the richness of the spiritual friendship Joy and I shared but also of the loving relationship I enjoyed with God through Jesus Christ. Many times as I struggled with my writing, I pictured Jesus sitting so close by in that chair, nodding and smiling at me, urging me on and encouraging me not to give up. How wonderful that an old chair Joy would in all likelihood have had to throw out could continue to minister to me in such a way!

I did not see Joy at all in the early months of 2011. I wanted to give her time to settle into her new home and work through the grief of having left such a huge part of her life behind her. We stayed in contact by phone and email and I knew her daughters were caring for her, helping her get organised, unpacking things, staying with her, taking her away on holidays. As well, I was busy again with speaking engagements and with editing my fifth novel, *Heléna's Legacy*, which had been accepted for publication towards the end of the previous year. Besides that, it was difficult for me to drive up to see Joy in those months because of severe pain from an old back problem. Joy did not want me to do anything that would exacerbate this, so while we would have loved to see each other, we had to be patient.

Some months earlier, I had begun work on my sixth novel, *The Inheritance*, a story focused on the destruction that hypocrisy, bitterness and lack of forgiveness can bring. I loved this story and felt it was my most powerful yet, but it had been a struggle to keep the momentum going because of the many interruptions I had experienced. I managed to complete it at last—but where to from there? I wanted to keep writing, but once again was unsure what direction God wanted me to take. Did God perhaps want me to become more involved in ministry in the local church we were now attending instead? Already I had been invited to give some input on mentoring and train others in this. I knew I could do it—I had plenty of material at hand and was experienced in mentoring. But was that where I should focus my energies?

I poured out my heart to Joy about this one day on the phone. It was still so good to be able to share such things with her and know she would respond in a caring, godly way. As we talked, it became clear my deepest desire was still to write. But, for some odd reason, I again felt guilty about giving in to this desire, wondering if God wanted me to do something more strategic or 'normal'. Joy listened, asking questions to help me clarify the issues involved. It had never been her way to tell me what to do—she respected me enough to believe I could hear God for myself and make my own decisions. Yet this occasion turned out to be different.

'But you *must* write!' she told me when I had finished—and that was that.

Later that day, I realised she was right. I had known it all along in my heart and had not forgotten the strong challenge God had given me to keep writing as I coloured in my purple Celtic pattern. Yet for some reason, I had still needed that little word of permission from Joy. Already a wild idea had come to me for my next book. It would be a risk—and I would need to think and pray long and hard about it—but I wanted to do it with all my heart.

In other conversations and emails during these months, I took great delight in telling Joy about some experiences I had when speaking at various places. I knew she would see many things in the same light as I did and appreciate hearing of God's hand at work in and through me, often in such unexpected ways. I had continued to report back to my email prayer team each time I spoke somewhere and Joy always read these, but I loved telling her extra little details and being encouraged by her responses. After one particular speaking engagement at an RSL Club where I had spoken to a war widows' group, I phoned Joy to tell her what had happened. As the women came to chat and buy books afterwards, I was surprised how many wanted to talk about their faith in God and about going to church—even more than the topic on which I had spoken. I had mentioned how I had served on a ministry team and that my husband was a minister, which seemed to capture their interest.

'They stayed talking for so long, I had to remind myself I was speaking to a secular group,' I told Joy. 'I almost found myself offering to pray for one of the women, but then realised it might not be the thing to do in that setting.'

We talked again about how strange it was in one way to make any division between the 'sacred' and the 'secular'. God was at work in people's lives wherever they were, as Joy reminded me and as I had sensed myself. She urged me again to keep finding such opportunities to speak and share about my writing in a natural way—and to expect God to minister to people, whatever the setting.

I went on then to tell her about one well-dressed and outspoken woman who had been the last to leave. She had insisted on buying a copy of *Jenna*, even though I felt *Laura* would be more suitable for her to read. A few days later, this lady phoned me, having found my number on the business card I had given her. She had opened her copy of *Jenna* and seen Joy's poem, '*You ask a drink of me a woman*', with Joy's name below it.

'Tell me,' she demanded, 'is Joy's husband's name David? And was her father a minister?'

It turned out this lady had grown up with Joy at a large church on Sydney's north shore, where Joy's father had ministered for many years. I was amazed when I remembered how certain this lady had been that she needed to buy *Jenna* rather than *Laura*. If she had listened to me, she would never have seen Joy's poem. I was also delighted to know that at least one person had read the poem and wondered how many more had been comforted or challenged by it. I hoped and prayed there were many.

At last, in June that year, I arranged to visit Joy in her new home. I was looking forward to our time together, not only because I would see her new villa, but also because I wanted to tell her about my idea for my next book. I was beginning to get excited about it, but knew I would need Joy's approval to proceed any further.

It seemed strange to drive up the mountains and turn left under the railway line instead of right at the corner service station, as I had done for so many years, to get to Joy's home. I drove slowly along her street, wondering what her row of villas looked like. And then I saw her, standing in a driveway looking out for me, smiling and waving. And soon I was stepping into her beautiful, new home, gazing around me with delight and not a little envy. It felt so right for Joy—and exactly the sort of villa I myself longed to own one day.

'I must bring my husband up to visit you, Joy,' I told her, laughing. 'This is just the sort of villa I'd like us to buy!'

Before we sat down for our usual cup of Lady Grey tea and biscuits, Joy showed me round with pride. I noticed many pieces of furniture from Joy's old home in the lounge area, including David's old grandfather clock against one wall. The kitchen and dining room were bright and airy, with windows and glass doors overlooking a small garden area at the rear. It was special to walk outside with Joy and see her delight at the new plants already growing there that her daughters had helped her put in. She also showed me various ones she had managed to bring with her from her old garden and how they seemed to be thriving in their new setting. Plans were afoot too, she told me, for more garden area to be established, once the warmer weather came. It was wonderful to see her so content and at peace in her new home and enjoying making it her own.

Joy then showed me around inside. On the divan in the spare bedroom, I noticed an intricate Turkish cushion cover I had brought back for her one year from the Grand Bazaar in Istanbul. I was touched she loved it enough to put it where she had. We returned to the lounge and, as I looked around, I saw some of Joy's pictures and other beautiful objects I had loved from her old study now very much at home in their new setting. A fascinating arrangement of autumn leaves on a polished, wooden cabinet nearby also caught my eye. And there, too, was a candle ready to be lit, just as I remembered from our times of sitting together in her study.

As we sipped our tea, I handed over a copy of my fifth novel, *Heléna's Legacy,* which had arrived from the printer only a few days earlier. As usual, Joy wanted to pay for it, but I insisted she accept it as a gift. After all, she had been so much a part of my whole writing journey and of keeping me faithful to God's call on my life to write.

'I'm not planning on having a launch this time,' I explained to her, 'but if you feel up to it, I'd love to take you out for lunch somewhere today to have our own little celebration. It would also be a way of celebrating your move to your new home too!'

There was plenty to catch up on over the next hour, but then I knew it was time to share my idea for my next book. I had mentioned it to Joy before, but now I wanted to make sure she was happy with the project.

'Joy, have you heard of the book by Mitch Albom called *Tuesdays with Morrie?*'[45] I asked her. 'Someone gave me a copy a while back and I really enjoyed reading it.'

Joy nodded. She had read it too and loved it.

'The moment I began reading it, the thought came to me that I could write something along those lines about our own friendship over all these years,' I continued. 'Of course, in many ways it would be quite different, but that book has inspired me to try.'

'But ... do you think there'd be enough to write about?' Joy asked in a doubtful voice.

'I don't know yet,' I laughed. 'I think there would be—I still have my journals from my college years and long after that, too. Often when I came to see you, I would jot down notes as we talked—do you remember? Then I would write them out again at home, so I have a record of many of the things we talked about and some of the comments you made. But ... would you be happy with the idea? It wouldn't be your biography—or mine. It would be a kind of memoir about our journey together in the past few years.'

Joy looked a little unsure but seemed happy as ever to support me.

'I'm not sure I know what you'd find to write about, but ... well, it sounds interesting. Do you think the DVDs of the interviews David and I did together a while back about our lives would be any help? You're quite free to borrow them if you'd like.'

My heart leapt at the idea, but at that stage, while the general concept of the book was clear, its specific content was still vague in my mind.

'Thanks for the offer,' I responded. 'Perhaps I'll leave it for now, but when I see you again, I should have a much clearer idea what further information I need. I don't know if it will work at all—but I'd like to try. I sense God could be in this.'

We then drove to Leura for lunch. Joy showed me a little, secluded restaurant away from the main street where we both enjoyed a wonderful, rustic-type meal. We chatted on, savouring the moment together. I had never had the opportunity to take Joy out for a meal before and felt so privileged to share this experience.

The next day, I received an email from her, commenting on how good it was to see me again and how much she had enjoyed our meal together. She had started reading my new novel, she wrote, and also mentioned how 'intrigued' she was about my non-fiction book idea. I felt relieved—at least she did not seem too put off by the concept. I would need to be careful, however, to ensure Joy was happy with everything I included about her, I realised, and to write about our relationship with the highest integrity.

Two weeks later, I received another email from her about *Heléna's Legacy* which also relieved and encouraged me:

> *Dear Jo-Anne*
> *After several startings and stoppings for various reasons, I*

*reached the stage that I couldn't put your book down. Just
loved it. It really ministered to me in several ways, about
which I'll speak to you some time. Thank you so much, dear
friend. I am sure it will be a blessing to many people.
Much love, Joy.*

I hoped and prayed even then that my non-fiction book that was
beginning to grip my heart would minister to her, too, and that she
would love it even more. Now I could see more clearly where I was
heading with it and was eager to drive up to visit her again as soon as
possible.

I was able to do so again towards the end of that month. But before
I did, three things happened that served to confirm I had made the
right decision in attempting to write about our relationship. The first
occurred as I was reading some verses in John 21 where the risen Jesus
calls out to his disciples in their boat, asking them if they have caught
any fish. He then instructs them to throw their nets on the right side
of the boat instead. They do—and end up with more fish than they can
handle. It seemed God was speaking straight to me as I read, urging me
to try to write something different this time and throw myself into this
non-fiction work.

The second came hard on the heels of the first in the form of an
email from a Christian writer friend. She wrote saying how excited she
was at my concept for my next book and how important she sensed it
was for me to write it. Then the third occurred when my husband and
I were invited to lunch by some old friends. When I mentioned I was
thinking of writing a work of non-fiction, the wife burst out:

'Oh, that's so interesting! I almost contacted you the other day to
say I felt you should be writing non-fiction!'

The day I visited Joy, I was hampered by severe lower back pain so
could not stay as long as I had planned. Nevertheless, we still chatted
for some time. Then Joy handed over her set of six precious DVDs,
'*Memory Moments*',[46] that she and David had managed to complete
before David became too ill. It was well timed from my perspective,

since in the following weeks I had to spend many hours lying down instead of at my desk. And as I began watching these DVDs, I soon realised what a treasure had been placed at my disposal. They revealed to me so many interesting things I had never known about Joy—and David—and enabled me to understand much better how Joy had become the wise, godly woman she had always been for me.

I was surprised and touched when, in the midst of viewing the final DVD, I heard my own name mentioned, in answer to a question about Joy's journey in spiritual companioning.

'I have a special friend, Jo-Anne Berthelsen,' I heard Joy explain. *'Jo-Anne felt called to study theology ... and it was a great joy, when she had to have spiritual direction regularly during her course, that she asked me. ... That has gone on for a number of years now—and I think we must be mutually blessed!'*

As I listened, I became even more determined to do justice to Joy in whatever I wrote.

Chapter Eighteen

Passing the Baton

I sit here in my study, collecting my thoughts after a mentoring session with a wonderful, young woman who serves on the ministry team of a nearby church. We have talked for over two hours, which is not surprising when there is so much happening in her life she needs to share. Before she came, I found some articles that might be helpful in making a particular decision she will soon need to make. I also prayed for her and checked over my notes from our last meeting. We had emailed each other since her previous visit and she had been very much in my thoughts and prayers as she tackled some difficult issues at her church.

Yet again this morning I have been so impressed with her maturity well beyond her years, her self-awareness and the careful way she thinks and prays through the key ministry matters confronting her. It was a privilege to listen as she made herself comfortable in Joy's old chair and shared her heart with me. I also noted her compassion for those in her church who need extra support right now, and her willingness to give of herself above and beyond what could be expected. Now I jot down a few more notes from our meeting together and pray for her again. I believe in her. I admire her pastoral ministry gifts and also her intellectual ability as she completes her college training. However, I fear for her a little as far as her future in her denomination is concerned. After all, she is a young woman in a male dominated environment. I pray her church will value her as they should and see her full potential. What a wonderful asset she would be on a ministry team anywhere, I think to myself yet again.

I reflect, too, on another young woman I have seen in recent days. I will see her only a few times, I know, in my role as her supervisor for a pastoral care course she has undertaken. But again, I can see such natural giftedness in her for this ministry and feel privileged to play even a small part in her current training. She has taken some years to find her niche in ministry, but now as a young mother she knows what God has called her to do and is determined to complete her course, despite having to fit studies around work and family. I pray for her as she comes to mind, that God will grant her the desire of her heart and provide a role where all her gifts can be utilised.

My mind then turns to another gifted woman in her early forties who has recently requested to meet with me for mentoring. She lives at a distance, so we meet at a shopping centre somewhat closer for her than my home. As I get to know her, I find myself thinking of Joy again and the things she would say to my new friend. Even at this early stage of our relationship, I suspect Joy would say in her gentle way, 'Be kind to yourself! Listen to your body!' My friend is so committed to working alongside her husband in his ministry role in a local church. She is putting all her energies into raising up new leaders and reaching out to those who do not as yet seem to have any faith in God—and my heart goes out to her. I think of the many hours Joy has listened to me over the years and I know I need to pass on what I have learnt.

In the past few years, advances in technology have made it possible for me to keep in contact with two other wonderful women serving

God overseas. My friend in Turkey and I have known each other for many years. I began to meet with her in a mentoring role around fifteen years ago—and here we still are, now touching base at regular intervals via Skype, smiling at each other courtesy of webcams and relating as best we can, despite the tyranny of distance. I am aware of her situation, having visited her five times now in her adopted country. I have just received another email from her and now lift her up to God. She is going through a discouraging time and I ask God to comfort and renew her. I have believed in her over all these years and will continue to do so, whether she stays where she is or comes home. And again I reflect what a wonderful, gifted woman she is, so committed to serving God and to sharing God's love with those around her.

My other Skype contact is equally gifted and committed. Along with her husband, she served elsewhere in Europe before relocating to the Netherlands. Now she balances training and caring for other workers from their organisation with ministry involvement in a fast-growing local church. I have mentored her for only a short while, but already I am in awe of her many gifts and what she has achieved, in the midst of caring for her teenage children. I look forward to following more of her journey and feel privileged to be able to share in it in some small way.

I let my mind wander, allowing memories of other women I have mentored in the past to surface. Some I have lost track of and wish I knew how they were faring. But others, I know, are serving God in amazing ways and have stood firm, despite the many challenges they have faced. I think of one girl, a gifted musician and worship leader, now the mother of three young children, still faithfully using her gifts in a large, vibrant church led by her pastor husband. I remember another, so gifted in youth and children's ministry, now married with a child of her own, and a vital part of this same church. Memories surface, too, of a girl who loved me to pray for her whenever we met during her difficult years of studying and of dealing with an unhappy marriage. I think of her now and honour her in my heart for how she has gone on in her life, learning to serve God in strategic ways through prayer ministry, as well as her chosen career of nursing.

Others come to mind as well—a young mother recently returned from overseas service with her husband and family; a quiet girl longing to be married, now with a loving husband and child; an older woman with outstanding intellectual and organisational ability who has overcome one disappointment after another in her determination to be the woman in ministry God has called her to be. I have loved and believed in them all—and even now feel privileged to have been part of their journey.

Yet I wonder—would I ever have experienced the privilege of mentoring these women, both past and present, had it not been for Joy's influence in my life? Yes, I undertook a mentor training course while at college and beyond, gaining much from it. And in the years that followed, I wrote and implemented my own mentoring program in our local church and co-wrote another to be used in a much larger church. But I know in my heart I would not have been so committed to the mentoring process and believed as much in its great value without having experienced such a positive mentoring relationship of my own with Joy. No training course could take the place of someone who modelled to me a way of caring for and believing in others that I was determined to emulate in my own ministry. I did not have to look far, I had discovered, to find younger and older women who longed for a spiritual companion such as I had in Joy. And more often than not, it had seemed so right for me to walk the journey with them, committing myself to the task, just as Joy did for me.

As I meet with those I now mentor, I smile whenever I remember a phrase or pass on a concept that I learnt from Joy. Often, as I reach for a book from the shelves in my study—perhaps even a book Joy recommended to me—I picture that small study in Joy's old home yet again and remember how blessed I was to have her share such resources with me. I glance around my study now, noting the many tangible reminders of Joy I can see. Like her, I have desired to make this room a warm, welcoming, safe space for any who come to share with me—a place where they can sense God's grace and know they will be accepted, whatever dark things might be brought to the light. I smile as I see on my walls the various pictures and quotations so reminiscent of those I remember at Joy's—some wise words from Teresa of Avila, a cross-stitched quotation from Emerson, the framed photograph of 'my' angel from the domed ceiling of St Paul's Cathedral, a card featuring the words Joy and I had laughed about together: '*She who trims herself to suit everybody will soon whittle herself away*'. Pot plants stand on a bookshelf near my windows to make up for the lack of the garden I had always admired outside Joy's study windows. And nearby on my desk is a unique and fascinating candle, given to me by the young woman who had sat beside it in Joy's old chair that very morning. Again I realise how much of Joy's way of spiritual companioning I have unconsciously imbibed.

I turn to my computer again and find an email from a wonderful, vibrant, Christian author friend who often contacts me, not only for spiritual encouragement but also for advice about her own writing. This time, I find her email particularly moving:

> *Hi Jo-Anne*
>
> *I just wanted to thank you for being there for me as I go through my ups and downs. I really appreciate the way you reply to my emails and give such thoughtful and wise responses, and always believe in me, even when I don't believe in myself. You really reflect the love of God to me and inspire me to be like this to other people too, even though it seems to be quite a rare quality to find in people. Thank you so much for that.*

I feel unworthy of the confidence she shows in me, yet she is right in that I believe in her, not only as a Christian but also as a writer. She is able, in my opinion, to put truths about God in a way that is so accessible for everyone, believer or not. And for a fleeting moment, I reflect on the fact that her email has put into words so well the very same things I have tried on occasions to say to Joy in a card or email.

And so Joy's ministry of spiritual companioning continues both to me and, I hope and pray, through me to others—both those I have mentored in the past and those with whom I now meet. On a tree at David and Joy's old home in the mountains hangs a rustic plaque containing the following words:

One generation plants the tree; the next sits in its shade.

Joy has planted so many seeds in my life. Time after time I have received the peace and wisdom and encouragement these have afforded me as they have grown within and found a home there. She has stretched her faith and her love and her belief in me over my spirit like the strong branches of one of those wonderful trees in her old garden and I have benefited so much from resting in their shade. Yet, while I know that resting place is still there for me, I realise I need to continue providing that same shade for others—for that next generation who will do wonderful things for God in this world well beyond my understanding and ability. And as they themselves grow and mature even further, may the day come when they too provide that shade and nurture for others, just as Joy has for me.

May it be so, Lord! May those who have been blessed through the company of faithful spiritual friends and mentors in turn walk that journey with others who long for such a one to come alongside them and uphold them. And may those who feel that longing be guided by you as they reach out and find that one sent from you who will stand with them and believe in them, providing a shady place for them to rest, to regain their strength and then to press on to be all you have called them to be.

May it be so, Lord!

Amen.

ENDNOTES

1   Camp Farthest Out is an interdenominational organisation that hosts Christ-centred, prayer-filled retreats for spiritual renewal. The purpose of these is to provide an environment in which Christians can spend time in worship, prayer and fellowship and thus strengthen their faith.

2   *All shall be well and all shall be well and all manner of thing shall be well.* These words come from the writings of **Julian of Norwich** (c. November 8, 1342 – c. 1416) who was an English mystic. She is called Julian after the Church of St Julian in Norwich, Norfolk, England where she lived as an anchoress in a cell attached to the church. At thirty years of age, when suffering from a severe illness, she had a series of visions which she recorded soon after. Then, having reflected on them for twenty years, she wrote an expanded version called *Revelations of Divine Love.*

3   Nouwen, Henri, *Out of Solitude*, Ave Maria Press, Indiana, 1974. Henri Nouwen (1932 – 1996), a Dutch Catholic priest, wrote over forty books on the spiritual life. He was ordained in 1957 and studied psychology at the Catholic University of Nijmegen in the Netherlands. In 1964 he moved to the United States to study at the Menninger Clinic. Nouwen later taught at the University of Notre Dame, and the Divinity Schools of Yale and Harvard. For several months during the 1970s, he lived with the Trappist monks in the Abbey of the Genesee, and in the early 1980s with the poor in Peru. In 1985 he was called to

join L'Arche in Trosly, France, the first of over a hundred communities founded by Jean Vanier for people with developmental disabilities. The following year, Henri Nouwen made his home at L'Arche Daybreak near Toronto, Canada.

4   Ignatian retreats can be of varying lengths and are based on the Spiritual Exercises of St Ignatius Loyola, the founder of the Catholic Jesuit Order.

5   Elijah House Ministries serves the wider Christian community by offering teaching, training and prayer ministry to bring restoration to broken lives and relationships. This ministry is based on biblical principles and on how God's laws impact our lives. It was founded in the US by John and Paul Sandford in 1974 and is now worldwide.

6   From the poem *Hertha* by Algernon Charles Swinburne (1837 – 1909).

7   Leunig, Michael, 'God help us to find our confession' in *When I talk to you: A cartoonist talks to God*, HarperCollins Australia, 2004.

8   From a brief poem known as Teresa of Avila's 'Bookmark' poem because it was found in her prayer book after her death. Different translations from the Spanish exist - another common translation of these lines is: *Let nothing disturb you; let nothing frighten you. All things are passing. God never changes.* Saint Teresa of Avila (1515 – 1582) was born in Avila, Spain. She founded the Order of the Discalced Carmelites and was canonized by Gregory XV in 1622.

9   Nouwen, Henri, *The Road to Daybreak*, UK, Darton, Longman and Todd, 1997.

10   Goudge, Elizabeth, *The Scent of Water*, UK, Coward-McCann, 1963. Elizabeth Goudge was an English novelist who was born in 1900 in Wells, England and died in 1984. She also wrote short stories and children's books. Her father was a minister and theology lecturer and Elizabeth's books contain Christian themes such as persevering through suffering, coming to faith in God and sacrifice. Many of her own life experiences are woven into her novels, as well as her great love for the English countryside.

11   Madeleine L'Engle (1918 – 2007) was an American Christian author of adult and young adult fiction, children's books, poetry and non-fiction,

including prayers, devotional writing and memoir. She was linked closely with the Episcopal Cathedral of St John the Divine in New York for many years as its librarian. As well as her strong interest in Christian themes, she was also fascinated by modern science. Among her most famous books are the young adult, award winning novel *A Wrinkle in Time*, her biographical *Crosswicks Journals* and her *Walking on Water: Reflections on Faith and Art*.

12 Gendlin, Eugene T, *Focusing*, New York, Bantam 1981 Rev Ed.

13 The Myers-Briggs Type Indicator is a questionnaire developed from the psychological type theories of Jung and is designed to measure the different ways people see the world and make decisions. The questions focus on four sets of opposite 'preferences'—Extrovert (E) and Introvert (I); Sensing (S) and Intuitive (N); Thinking (T) and Feeling (F); Judging (J) and Perceiving (P)—thus giving a possible sixteen personality or psychological types.

14 Hurley, K V and Dobson, T E, *What's My Type?: Use the Enneagram System of Nine Personality Types to Discover 'Your Best Self'*, San Francisco, HarperCollins/Enneagram Resources, 1991.

15 Leunig, Michael, *The Curly Pyjama Letters*, Melbourne, Viking/Penguin Books, 2001, p 26.

16 Rizza, Margaret, *Fountain of Life: Music for Contemplative Worship* Kevin Mayhew 1997.

17 See Dawna Markova's website www.dawnamarkova.com.

18 For more information about the Aquinas Academy in Sydney's Rocks area, see www.aquinas-academy.com.

19 For more about existential psychologist Rollo May's life and writings, see Dr C George Boeree's article at webspace.ship.edu/cgboer/may.html.

20 Chittister, Joan, *Scarred by Struggle, Transformed by Hope*, Grand Rapids, Eerdmans, 2003.

21 Kelly, Thomas, *A Testament of Devotion*, New York, Harper, 1941.

22 Murray, Craufurd, *Cherishing Christ : Journeying with Christ through the Seasons*, NZ, Craufurd Murray, 2003.

23 L'Engle, Madeleine, *Walking on Water: Reflections on Faith and Art*, New York, Bantam, 1982.

24 Ibid, p 149.

25 Ibid, p 109.

26 Yancey, Philip, *Soul Survivor*, London, Hodder and Stoughton, 2001, pp 253 – 254.

27 Elizabeth Goudge, *The Joy of the Snow*, London, Coward, McCann & Geoghegan, 1974.

28 Irenaus was one of the early church fathers and became the Bishop of Lyons. He was born in the first half of the second century in 130AD or possibly earlier, and died around 202AD. He was a theologian and apologist, his most famous work being *Against Heresies*, written to refute the teachings of Gnosticism.

29 de Mello, Anthony, *Awareness: The Perils and Opportunities of Reality*, New York, Image Books, 1990.

30 Thoreau, Henry David, *Walden*, a reflection on simple living written in 1854.

31 Cameron, Julia, *The Artist's Way: A Course in Discovering and Recovering your Creative Self*, London, Pan, 1995.

32 'Little Gidding' is the name of the final poem in a set of four entitled *Four Quartets* by T S Eliot, published in 1942. Little Gidding, a village in Cambridgeshire, England, was the home of an old Anglican religious community.

33 L'Engle, Madeleine, *Glimpses of Grace: Daily Thoughts and Reflections*, with Carole F Chase, San Francisco, Harper, 1998, p 68.

34 See eg O'Donohue, John, *Anam Cara: Spiritual Wisdom from the Celtic World*, London, Bantam, 1999.

35 See eg Newell, J Philip, *Listening for the Heartbeat of God*, New York, Paulist Press, 1997.

36 See eg de Waal, Esther, *The Celtic Way of Prayer: The Recovery of the Religious Imagination*, London, Hodder and Stoughton, 1996.

37 Young, William P *The Shack*, Los Angeles, Windblown Media, 2007.

38 Kahlil Gibran (1883 – 1931) was a Lebanese poet, writer and artist from a Maronite Catholic family who migrated to the USA when he was a young man. His most well-known work is *The Prophet*, a book of essays written in 1923 and published by Knopf. While his works display a strong

Christian influence, they also show other influences such as Islam, Sufism and theosophy.

39 Benner, David, *The Gift of Being Yourself: The Sacred Call to Self-Discovery*, Downers Grove, IVP, 2004.

40 Barna, George and Viola, F *Pagan Christianity? Exploring the Roots of Our Church Practices*, BarnaBooks, 2002.

41 Viola, Frank, *Reimagining Church: Pursuing the Dream of Organic Christianity*, Colorado Springs, David C Cook, 2008.

42 Jacobsen, Wayne, and Coleman, David, *So You Don't Want to Go to Church Anymore? An Unexpected Journey*, Los Angeles, Windblown Media, 2006.

43 Frost, Michael, *Exiles: Living Missionally in a Post-Christian Culture*, Peabody, Hendrickson, 2006.

44 This poem, commonly called 'The Gate of the Year' was written by Minnie Louise Haskins (1875-1957). It was published under the title 'God Knows' in a collection called 'The Desert' in 1908. It was quoted by King George VI in his Christmas broadcast in 1939, after Queen Elizabeth had given him a copy, and was also read out at her funeral in 2002.

45 Albom, Mitch, *Tuesdays with Morrie: an old man, a young man, and life's greatest lesson*, Sydney, Hachette Australia, 2007.

46 *Memory Moments: videos that tell your life story ...* are produced by Laurel and Ross Wraight, Pendle Hill, NSW.

About the author

Jo-Anne Berthelsen lives in Sydney but grew up in Brisbane. She holds degrees in Arts and Theology and has worked as a high school teacher, editor and secretary, as well as in local church ministry. Jo-Anne is passionate about touching hearts and lives through both the written and spoken word. She is the author of five published novels – *Heléna, All the Days of My Life, Laura, Jenna* and *Heléna's Legacy,* with a sixth, *The Inheritance,* due for release in 2013. Jo-Anne loves music, reading, mentoring younger women, and sharing with community groups about writing. She is married to a retired minister and has three grown-up children and three grandchildren. For more information about Jo-Anne or to contact her, please visit her website, www.jo-anneberthelsen. com.